4/92

MOTHER EARTH ....

Other works by Martin Duberman

AN
EPIC
DRAMA
OF
EMMA
GOLDMAN'S
LIFE

MOTHER
EARTH

MARTIN DUBERMAN

ST. MARTIN'S PRESS NEW YORK

For Kent Paul
who believed in this play,
and rescued it

MOTHER EARTH: AN EPIC DRAMA OF EMMA GOLDMAN'S LIFE. Copyright ©
1991 by Martin Duberman. All rights reserved. Printed in the
United States of America. No part of this book may be used or
reproduced in any manner whatsoever without written permission except in the case of brief quotations embodied in critical
articles or reviews. For information, address St. Martin's
Press, 175 Fifth Avenue, New York, N.Y. 10010.

Designed by Dawn Niles

Library of Congress Cataloging-in-Publication Data

Duberman, Martin B.
    Mother earth : an epic drama of Emma Goldman's life /
Martin Duberman.
        p.   cm.
    ISBN 0-312-05954-X
    1. Goldman, Emma, 1869–1940.   2. Anarchists—United
States--Biography.   I. Title.
    HX843.7.G65D83   1991
    335'.83'092—dc20
    [B]   90-26939
                                                              CIP

First Edition: July 1991

10 9 8 7 6 5 4 3 2 1

PREFACE ....

This play was originally commissioned in the early seventies by the New York PBS affiliate. The station had approached me to write a teleplay on the life of Susan B. Anthony but I had fervently resisted that idea, urging them to substitute for that "dray horse of the suffrage movement" the far more dramatic figure of Emma Goldman. The PBS people had never heard of Goldman—she was not, in the early seventies, nearly as well known as she is today—and I had to mount my soapbox.

I told them Emma (years of heroine-worshipping her had put us, in my heart, on a first-name basis) had led a life of high-pitched intensity and incorruptible devotion to anarchist principles that had made her all at once a passionate opponent of traditional authority, a staunch feminist, and an eloquent advocate of sexual liberation. Hers was an operatic life that naturally lent itself to dramatic treatment. The astonishment, I said, was that no one had previously put that life on the stage or on film.

In the early seventies it was still possible to argue that a principled, radical figure would have resonance for millions of Americans and was therefore suitable fare for television. This is not to say that the powers that be at PBS were easily persuaded, but only that ultimately they did yield to my arguments, junking the Susan B. Anthony project and authorizing me to prepare a script on the life of Emma Goldman. In the proverbial fever of excitement, I completed the teleplay within a few months. I named it *Mother Earth,* in memory of Emma's influential magazine, and to signify my own sense of her primordial nature.

On the very day I finished the script, I got a pained call from a PBS executive. He had just had news from Washington that the station's budget was being slashed to discourage what in President Nixon's mind had been its "excessively radical" programming. Since *Mother Earth* was not yet in production and seemed the most radical of the pending shows, PBS had regretfully decided—though no one had yet read my script—that it was the logical candidate for cancellation. Mumbling something apologetic about "maybe in the future," PBS told me I was free to sell the play elsewhere.

Instead, deeply disheartened, I put the manuscript in the recesses of my refrigerator—the place where I temporarily store all my unpublished or unproduced work as a forlorn safeguard against fire. In the upshot, this temporary expedient lasted more than ten years: I simply hadn't the stomach for peddling the script. Then, in the mid-eighties, a director friend, Kent Paul, asked me one day if I had any unproduced material he might consider for the stage. After reading *Mother Earth,* he enthusiastically urged me to attempt a revision and to let him try to arouse interest in a production.

Kent felt the ideal format for *Mother Earth* would be as a long theater piece, perhaps presented in two parts on alternate nights—a style pioneered in the Royal Shakespeare Company's production of *Nicholas Nickelby*. Another possibility would be to present the script as a television miniseries, broken into three or four segments. I expressed willingness, should neither of these preferred options arouse interest, to condense the play into a single two-hour version suitable for more standard stage or TV presentation.

Everyone Kent and I showed the script to over the next few years—we approached perhaps a half-dozen managements—had praise for it, but no one wanted to produce it. "Too ambitious" and "too radical" were the standard reasons for rejection. Convinced though I was of the importance of covering Emma's entire life in order to convey its epic sweep, and of the equal importance of not trimming on her politics, I was willing to abridge the play and did offer several pared-down versions. But they had no takers either. Even in shortened form, Emma Goldman's audacious life, by the eighties, had little appeal in a cultural climate that had become deeply conservative.

So back into the refrigerator went *Mother Earth*. The play's appearance here in printed form is due not to the interest of theatrical producers in its dramatic or political potential, but to the belief of my editor, Michael Denneny, and St. Martin's Press, that the script has literary merit. I am grateful for even that partial vote of confidence, and have revised *Mother Earth* yet again for this volume. To help the reader (as opposed to a viewer) of this printed version, I have broken the text into three acts.

My effort to tell Emma Goldman's story in dramatic form is neither the first nor last time I've tried to put history on the stage. My first produced play, *In White America*—which opened off Broadway in 1963—was an effort to tell, through historical documents, the story of being black in this country. And in my most recent (1990) play, *Posing Naked*, I've continued to turn to the past—this time to the 1960 arrest of the literary critic, Newton Arvin, for purportedly running a pornography ring—for material that might illuminate the issues of state oppression and the permissible limits of sexual expression.

I have made many other attempts in the intervening years to make plays out of historical materials, and in the process my views on *how* history can or should be put on the stage have undergone considerable revision. Back in 1963 I held to an attitude of scholarly purity that verged on the fanatical. I refused to add one word to the script of *In White America* that did not come directly from a bona fide document, rigidly confining my own writing to brief bridges between scenes.

Yet I was well aware that in choosing some historical materials over others, and in then abridging them according to my own sense of what was "important" and "dramatic," I was engaging in a subjective process that could most certainly be described as a form of invention. Indeed, I wrote a long essay at the time, "History and Theater" (printed as an appendix to paperback editions of *In White America*), in which I argued that even the most scrupulous professional historians were inescapably involved in shaping the historical record in accordance with their own idiosyncratic values, however unconsciously held.

But back in 1963 I was closely wedded to the notion that, as a professional historian, my *primary* obligation was to reconstruct the past as objectively as possible, and, in the name of that goal, sharply to restrict my own imaginative interventions. Even as I cut and spliced historical diaries, letters, newspaper accounts, and congressional debates into "scenes," I chose to believe that the documentary format was successfully minimizing any opportunity to impose my own voice. And beyond what I accepted as an irreducible amount of minor contamination (such as a change in tense here or there), I would allow neither myself nor any of the actors to move an inch. Not a single word (nay, a comma!) could be omitted or inserted into the script that could not be found in the material I had "objectively" preselected.

This literal-mindedness got me into a running battle with one of the *In White America* actors (whom I'll call "Paul"). One of Paul's assignments was to read the bridge material introducing the John Brown scene in the play, material that included the line, "John Brown has alternately been called a saint and a madman." Paul, who is black, would have none of it. He angrily argued that the saint/madman phrase maligned a man who was a hero to African-Americans. And when I tried explaining to him that historians truly *did* divide in just that way in their verdict on Brown, he wanted to know how many of those historians were black. "Not many," I had to confess. Paul shrugged—and went right on omitting the offending line whenever I wasn't standing hawk-eyed in the back of the theater.

In the years since *In White America,* I've loosened up considerably, letting my imaginative needs, and the requirements of the dramatic form in which I was working, increasingly surface. Without ever losing my respect for evidence, and trying always to stay within its known boundaries, I've nonetheless been more willing than before to bend it a bit now and then (in *Mother Earth,* for example, I felt that for dramatic purposes I had to reverse the actual chronology of Emma's employment in Garson's factory and her arrival at Sachs's café in New York).

If my scrupulosity about evidence has persisted, I've learned over time to welcome enthusiastically its frequent absence from the historical record as an opportunity to substitute my own sense of what "actually" happened. In several of the plays I wrote during the 1970s, I simply expropriated an historical place—the battlefield at Gettysburg; the 19th century commune at Oneida—and used it as backdrop for characters, dialogue and plot that I mostly created out of whole cloth.

In another of my 1970s plays—about the Roman emperor Elagabalus—the historical record proved so scanty and disputed, that I felt no scruple at all in using it as a suggestive basis only for writing a kind of meditation on the recurring duel between state orthodoxy and individual nonconformity. And in my one-act play *The Recorder,* I tried to capture the process itself—contradictory and even mysterious—whereby we attempt to reconstruct the "truth" about the past.

When writing *Mother Earth* (and the same is true of my later play, *Visions of Kerouac*), I chose to interweave historical material with my own inventions to the point where I can no longer, at this remove in time, always be certain which words come from Emma Goldman herself and which are mine. Almost all the scenes and characters in *Mother Earth* are based on actual episodes and people in her life and some of the dialogue, as well, is taken directly from her own writings, letters, or speeches. But often, too, I simply let a phrase or a few lines from Emma trigger my own continuations—our contributions to the text becoming blurred in a way that, to me at least, satisfyingly represents the inspirational influence of her life on my own. Since the first draft of *Mother Earth* is now nearly twenty years old, it's unlikely I could any longer entirely disentangle the two voices even if I wanted to. But, irresponsibly, I do not want to.

ACKNOWLEDGMENTS

I am grateful to Susan Brownmiller, Michael Denneny, Frances Goldin, Kent Paul, and Eli Zal for their helpful comments in shaping the text; to Keith Kahla for a variety of assists; and to Candace Falk for photographs.

ACT ....
ONE

(FADE IN: A parade of feminists. A delegation marches by holding aloft the banner, THE EMMA GOLDMAN BRIGADE. *At the bottom of the frame, a date card:* MAY 20, 1991. *Date card changes to:* JUNE 27, 1934.)

VOICE-OVER (FEMALE):   Dearest Emma: Love and greetings on your sixty-fifth birthday. You to me, are the future they will, paradoxically, hark back to in time.

(FADE IN: to gangplank of the Buford, *tied up in port awaiting debarkation. Men and women, a forlorn lot, are making their way up the gangplank. Date card changes to:* DECEMBER 21, 1919. *A commotion at the foot of the gangplank as Emma Goldman and Alexander Berkman arrive and are immediately surrounded by a group of reporters.)*

FIRST REPORTER: Is there any last statement you'd like to make, Miss Goldman? Or you, Mr. Berkman?

BERKMAN: We made our statements at the trial.

EMMA: *(glancing up the gangplank)* You wouldn't want them to leave without us, would you?

FIRST REPORTER: You haven't lost your sense of humor.

EMMA: It comes and goes.

SECOND REPORTER: Are you bitter about President Wilson's deporting order?

BERKMAN: We're only two of some three hundred.

(Man on a stretcher is carried past them up the gangplank. Emma bends down to hug him and whisper a few words.)

EMMA *(to reporters)*:   The doctor says that *if* the journey is not longer than a month, he has a good chance of surviving. Though as you may have heard *(gesturing toward the ship)*, the "good ship *Buford*" was condemned by the United States government as unseaworthy.

THIRD REPORTER: Do you know your destination?

EMMA: No one will tell us. If *you* could enlighten us, we would be grateful.

THIRD REPORTER: They've told you nothing?

EMMA: They've told us a great deal. They've told us that we are "dangerous enemies" of the country, that we are lawless anarchists who have blasphemously denounced the tyrannies of church and state. To hold such opinions, they say, is madness; to *express* them, treason. But our destination? No, of that they have told us nothing.

THIRD REPORTER: The speculation is that it will be Russia.

BERKMAN: We hope it is Russia.

SECOND REPORTER: Your allegiance *is* with the Bolsheviks, isn't it, Miss Goldman?

EMMA: My allegiance is with people. I don't recognize the swollen pride of any nation.

SECOND REPORTER: Why do you hate America?

EMMA: Pardon me, sir, but you sound like a fool.

SECOND REPORTER: For twenty-five years you've railed against our government.

EMMA: For *thirty-five* years. Against *all* governments.

SECOND REPORTER: Then you do hate America.

EMMA: Sir, you *are* a fool. I will never stop loving this country. Longing for it . . . longing for its possibilities . . .

THIRD REPORTER: You're dressed awfully swell, for someone who claims to be poor and to hate capitalism.

EMMA: I am a multimillionaire—in friends.

FIRST REPORTER: Mr. Berkman, do you find any irony in the fact that Henry Clay Frick—the man you tried to assassinate thirty years ago—has died this very week?

BERKMAN: Thousands of people have died this week.

FIRST REPORTER: Oh, come now, Mr. Berkman.

EMMA: Alexander Berkman has paid his debt in full: fourteen years in your prisons. Henry Clay Frick has died with *his* debts unpaid.

SECOND REPORTER: Is that all you have to say about Frick?

5 • • •

BERKMAN: You can add: Mr. Frick has been deported by God.

(Emma and Berkman start up the gangplank.)

THIRD REPORTER *(calling after them)*:   This is the end of the line, Emma Goldman, isn't it?

EMMA: No. Only another beginning . . .

(The deportees, crowding the rails, start singing "The Internationale." The ship's whistle sounds.)

(CUT TO: Emma and Berkman take their places on the rail, their arms tightly interlocked. A guard grabs Berkman.)

GUARD: Male prisoners in steerage. Down below! Fast!*

(Emma and Berkman embrace. Emma clings to him.)

EMMA: Sasha . . . Sashenka . . .

BERKMAN: Now, now, old girl. It's only for a few weeks. We've endured years.

EMMA: Good-bye, old pal . . .

(Berkman is removed roughly. Emma stands at the rail, gazing out to sea. The Statue of Liberty appears in the background.)

(CUT TO: A CLOSE-UP of the Statue.)

(CUT TO: The ship's porthole. Visible in the porthole is the rapturous face of Emma Goldman as a young woman. She turns into the cabin excitedly.)

EMMA: Helena! Helena! I can see it! Come quick!

(Helena goes up to the porthole. The two girls press their faces against it.)

EMMA: Dear sister, at last!

HELENA: Did you think it would be *green*?

EMMA: Oh yes—everything!

(CUT TO: Crowded tenement street in New York City. Emma and Helena are lugging their cardboard suitcases. Emma is also carrying a sewing machine. They look exhausted. Emma suddenly points up at a building.)

EMMA: There! Number thirty-one!

HELENA: Oh, thank God . . .

EMMA: I told you we'd find it, silly. New York is no crazier than St. Petersburg.

HELENA: I've been hearing Papa's warning in my ears all day: The police will arrest you as "loose women."

EMMA: Papa! Papa! He thinks women are born to make gefüllte fish! And the *smartest* get to cut noodles.

(They are at the door to Number 31. Emma searches the nameplates.)

EMMA: Aha—Tanta Rosenzweig! We're here, Helena!

(They grab and hug each other. Emma pushes the apartment buzzer.)

EMMA: Tell Tanta I'll be back by nightfall.

HELENA *(flabbergasted)*:   You *what?*

EMMA *(beaming)*:   I've sworn to myself that the first door I'd enter in the New World would be—Sachs's Café.

(Excited noises from the top of the stairs.)

EMMA: They're coming. *(kisses Helena)* Two hours, dear sister . . .

HELENA: *Meshugana!* Just like Papa. *Meshugana!*

(Emma starts to leave, then hurries back and picks up the sewing machine to take with her.)

HELENA: What are you doing?

EMMA: It must never be out of my sight.

HELENA: It weighs two stone! You don't even know where Sachs's Café is!

EMMA *(holding up the machine)*:   Independence: light as a feather!

(She hurries off.)

(CUT TO: Sachs's Café. Emma is talking to the bartender. No one else is in the place, except for two men seated at one of the tables.)

EMMA: But I thought he came here *all* the time.

BARTENDER: Johann Most is a busy man, young lady.

EMMA: Emma Goldman is my name.

BARTENDER: Well, Miss Goldman, newspapers don't edit themselves.

EMMA: *Die Freiheit* has been my Bible. In Russia it passes from hand to hand. Johann Most is a hero in Russia. . . .

BARTENDER: Yes, so some say.

EMMA: *Some?*

BARTENDER: It's a small movement, but we wouldn't be anarchists if each was not his own leader, eh?

EMMA: Ah—so you're a comrade!

BARTENDER: This *is* Sachs's Café, Miss Goldman.

(*They laugh.*)

BARTENDER: And when did you get here from Russia?

EMMA: Today.

BARTENDER: *Today?* You've been here one day?

EMMA: Not all of it. We left Ellis Island this morning.

BARTENDER: Good God! (*calling out to the two men at the table*) Sasha! Fedya!

(*The two look up.*)

9 •••

BARTENDER: Come meet a new comrade. (to *Emma*) Do you know anyone in New York?

EMMA: An aunt. My sister came with me.

(Berkman and Fedya are at the bar.)

BARTENDER: Miss Goldman, this is Alexander Berkman, called by everyone, Sasha.

(Emma extends her hand forcefully.)

EMMA: How do you do, Sasha.

BERKMAN *(cold):*   How do you do, Miss Goldman.

BARTENDER: And this is Fedya Meyerman.

(Fedya makes a sweeping bow.)

FEDYA: I am deeply honored, Miss Goldman.

BERKMAN: Clown.

FEDYA *(mocking):*   A clown *and* a "spendthrift." You may as well know the worst at once, Miss Goldman.

(Emma flushes with pleasure.)

BARTENDER: Miss Goldman just arrived this morning. She's looking for Johann Most.

EMMA: Please, you must call me Emma. I am not formal.

(Fedya extends his arm.)

FEDYA: Well, Emma, come to our table.

BERKMAN: Why are you looking for Johann Most?

EMMA: Because I'm an anarchist. I want to work for the Cause.

FEDYA: Please, first some wine, then the Cause. (*leans down to take her sewing machine*) Here, let me take that.

EMMA: Why?

FEDYA (*surprised*):   Why?

EMMA: I'm strong. (*picks up the sewing machine*)

FEDYA (*joking*):   Aha—an emancipé. A *radicalke*! Sasha may like you yet.

EMMA: It's a sewing machine. It's how I made my living in St. Petersburg.

BERKMAN: I, too, am from St. Petersburg. It has given many brave sons to the revolution. Even a few daughters.

EMMA: My uncle Yegor was imprisoned in the Petro-Pavlovsky Fortress. For being an anarchist.

BERKMAN (*decisively*):   Come to the table.

(*DISSOLVE TO: The table. The three are in the middle of a conversation.*)

EMMA: My sister also sews. We hope to start a cooperative dress shop. Like Vera in *What's To Be Done*. Meantime, I will get a job in a factory.

BERKMAN *(surprised)*: You've read Chernyshevsky? Impossible. His books are banned in Russia.

EMMA *(angry)*: I've read *all* the forbidden books: Chernyshevsky, Turgenev, Gontcharov. Yes, and I was accepted at the gymnasium—a girl, a Jewish girl, accepted at the gymnasium!

FEDYA: That's amazing, Emma!

EMMA *(reproachfully, at Berkman)*: My father didn't think girls should go to school.

FEDYA: Did you go?

EMMA: I told him I'd throw myself into the Neva if he refused to let me. He said, "The pig woman cheated me. You should have been a boy."

(They laugh, Berkman grudgingly.)

EMMA: I used to hope I'd come down with a terrible disease. I thought it might make father kind—like when he drinks wine on Succoth.

BERKMAN: I'm sorry if I hurt your feelings— Emma.

FEDYA *(yelling to the bartender)*: Wine, wine! To Succoth, and pig women, to Chernyshevsky and Vera!

BERKMAN: There's no money for wine.

EMMA: I have money. Five dollars! Can you buy food at Sachs's? I haven't eaten all day.

FEDYA: The best steak in New York, Emma—for *forty* cents!

EMMA: Then we can *all* have steak!

BERKMAN *(cold)*: I'm sure Fedya will join you.

EMMA: Aren't you hungry, Sasha?

BERKMAN: Give Fedya my forty cents. He'll buy flowers with it.

EMMA: I don't understand.

FEDYA: Sasha thinks I squander money on useless things: flowers, wine, oils and brushes for my painting.

EMMA: You're a painter! How marvelous, Fedya.

BERKMAN: An anarchist can't enjoy luxuries when the People are starving.

EMMA: Beautiful things are necessities, not luxuries.

FEDYA *(smiling)*: Ah! A "bourgeois" ally!

BERKMAN: There is only one necessity, and that is the Cause. It requires sacrifice. Fedya sacrifices *when convenient.*

EMMA: You sound like Rakhmetov in Chernyshevsky's novel. So single-minded.

BERKMAN: I thank you for the compliment.

FEDYA: Sasha is a true disciple of Johann Most—a man of "the deed."

BERKMAN: All means are justified in the war of humanity against its enemies.

FEDYA *(animated and serious)*: Violence will destroy anarchism. Anarchists are the champions of life. Most's philosophy of "the deed" is contempt for life.

BERKMAN: To commit the deed is to toss the stone which will start the avalanche. To remove a tyrant through assassination is to take one life in order to give life to the many.

EMMA: But even Johann Most says the deed should be the *last* resort—when there is no other way.

BERKMAN: Most is German.

FEDYA *(to Emma)*: Have you ever seen him?

EMMA: No.

FEDYA: He isn't exactly Romeo.

EMMA: Fedya!

FEDYA: Old. No jaw. His face all twisted. You said you liked beautiful things.

EMMA: Beauty isn't a physical property. I don't think like a shopgirl, Fedya.

BERKMAN *(to Emma):* You see what I mean. Do you want to meet Most? When he debates the socialist, Schleier at Ukrainian Hall, I will take you. Afterwards I'll introduce you. Most will make you understand the deed.

EMMA: I will meet Most?! I don't believe it! *(starts to get up)* I must tell my sister!

FEDYA: There's plenty of time. First have your steak.

(Berkman snorts in disgust.)

EMMA: Yes, we must all have steak—to celebrate. *(calls out to the bartender)* Steak for three!

FEDYA: And wine.

EMMA: And wine!

BERKMAN: I told you I'm not hungry.

EMMA: A strong man like you not hungry? Impossible. Please, Sasha. To help me celebrate!

FEDYA *(coaxing):* Eh, Sasha, come, come . . .

EMMA: Comrades are supposed to share, no? *Please,* Sasha.

(As Berkman scowls, CUT TO: The Buford (scene 1, 1919). Emma and her cabinmates are emptying out their suitcases.)

WOMAN: Underwear, too, Emma?

EMMA: Everything you don't need for immediate

use. Sasha says the conditions in steerage are unbelievable. The men are freezing. We must share everything. Sweaters, socks, underwear, *everything* . . .

WOMAN: I'm still surprised they let you see him.

EMMA: I told them I'd go on a hunger strike. . . . You should have seen Sasha's dear face. Lit up with energy. The men have chosen him to present the demands. He said to save what we can from our meals. Their food is so poor, the sick ones can't hold it down.

WOMAN: We're lucky by comparison.

EMMA: Always, dear Dora. (*laughs*) Women are thought to be the "delicate" ones.

(DISSOLVE TO: Garson's factory. Lunch break. Emma and other young women are eating noodle pudding from their paper bags. Emma is excitedly waving a newspaper at them.)

EMMA: But they're innocent men, *innocent!* Doesn't that matter to you?

FIRST WOMAN: So *you* say. Who knows.

EMMA (*slaps newspaper*):   Look! "Anarchists Throw Bomb in Haymarket Square. Reds Inaugurate Reign of Terror." Those men are *workers*, like us. They met in Haymarket to protest police brutality in breaking up their meeting.

SECOND WOMAN (*sympathetic*):   But *someone* threw a bomb, Emma. Five men *are* dead.

EMMA: "Someone." But *not* Parsons and Spies. They've been arrested because they are known leaders of the anarchist movement. I tell you, it's an excuse to break the movement! The state will hang all of them—mark my words.

FIRST WOMAN: You're so sure of everything.

SECOND WOMAN: My Fred says women shouldn't mix in politics.

FIRST WOMAN: Especially women new to the country. America is not Russia, you know.

EMMA: You may be right. . . . (*gesturing around her*) Eleven hours a day sewing overcoat belts . . . Two fifty a week in pay . . . It is *worse* here than in St. Petersburg. And there, at least, we could talk and sing. *And* go to the toilet without permission.

FIRST WOMAN: The police in Haymarket didn't kill themselves. Someone murdered them. And murderers should be hung.

(*Emma looks as if she might hit her; the second woman restrains her.*)

SECOND WOMAN: Tell Mr. Garson your complaints. He owns this factory. My noodle pudding's cold, with all the talk.

EMMA: Yes, why not Garson? . . .

(*She strides off angrily.*)

FIRST WOMAN (*calling after her*): If the government hangs them all it will be a service to decent people!

(CUT TO: Emma at the door to Garson's office. She's explaining to his secretary why she must see him.)

EMMA: Tell Mr. Garson it is urgent. It has to do with factory production. With a possible slowdown.

(The secretary looks dubious, but goes into the inner office. In a few seconds she reappears and nods for Emma to come in. Garson is at his desk. He doesn't look up or rise as Emma enters. A vase of American Beauty roses is on the desk.)

GARSON: Yes?

EMMA: What beautiful roses. *(he looks up, surprised)* I once tried to buy one in a flower shop. It cost a dollar—half my weekly salary.

GARSON: What is it you want?

EMMA: Yesterday Tanya Rosenbluth, who works the machine next to mine, fainted and fell to the floor.

GARSON: What is your name?

EMMA: Emma Goldman.

GARSON: I thought so. You're the one who insisted the foreman stop the machines.

EMMA: Tanya was very ill. I had to squeeze the juice of an orange from my lunch basket into her mouth.

GARSON: I've already had a full report of the episode. The girl was shamming. And you encouraged the sham, so the two of you could take the day off and idle in the park.

EMMA: I told the foreman to deduct from my pay. Tanya needed fresh air.

GARSON: And is he deducting for your time *now*?

EMMA: After room, board, and carfare, Mr. Garson, I have forty cents a week left over. I can never buy a book, hear a concert . . .

GARSON: None of my other girls complain. They, of course, are German. Russians are known for extravagance. Perhaps if you learned the importance of hard work, Miss Goldman, of . . .

(CUT TO: The vase of roses. Emma's hand comes down around the vase.)

GARSON *(voice-over):*   . . . the meaning of an honest dollar, of . . .

(CUT TO: Garson's face, eyes wide in amazement— just before the vase hits him.)

(As the CAMERA PULLS BACK out of the debris, we are in a room full of shouting people. Emma is being restrained by her sister, Helena. An empty pitcher is lying on the floor, water all around it. Emma's father is screaming abuse at her. A female guest cowers in the corner, being comforted by her husband. Emma's mother sits impassively in a chair.)

FATHER: How dare you attack a guest in our home?! Have you no shame, no respect?!

EMMA: *She* is the one with no respect. I warned her! I warned her not to talk that way about Perovskaya. Perovskaya is a saint, a martyr!

WOMAN: A murderer! There has never been a kinder czar than Alexandrovich.

EMMA: Kind to *you*, you who feed off the Russian people.

HUSBAND: *Meshumed . . . radicalke . . .*

FATHER *(shouting at Emma):* You are my disgrace! You will always be my disgrace! *(pushes her violently)* Wanton! You cannot be my child!

(Helena intervenes, tries to restrain her father.)

EMMA: I'm not your child. I'm no one's child.

FATHER: Out of this room—out!

EMMA: No—out of this *house*, now and forever!

(CUT TO: The girls' bedroom. Emma and Helena are packing.)

EMMA: You don't have to come with me, Helena. It's me he hates, not you.

HELENA: He's passionate, Emma. Like you. He cannot stand opposition from women.

EMMA: I will not be told what to do with my life. It's *mine*. And *I'll* lead it.

HELENA *(ironic)*:   If only you had agreed to let father marry you off last year.

EMMA *(indignant)*:   *Marry?* Sold like a piece of meat!

HELENA: He wasn't a bad man.

EMMA: He would have been a jailer, like all husbands. I have more to do with my life than knit shawls and cook kasha. A new world is coming, Helena. I'll find my people, my real people. . . .

(CUT TO: Ukrainian Hall. Johann Most and Schleier are in the midst of their debate. Most is in his mid-forties, of medium height, with a large head out of proportion to his body and a thick, steel gray head of hair. His face is deformed by a twisted jaw and a large swelling on the left side. He is autocratic and cold, yet charismatic—and a brilliant speaker: caustic, fluent, incisive. Most is talking.)

(CUT TO: Emma, Berkman, Fedya, and Helena in the audience. Emma's body is tense with excitement.)

MOST: . . . It is true that anarchists differ widely among themselves in their strategies for achieving the good society. But what makes us all anarchists is our agreement as to what the good society *is*. It is a society free of dictation. *That* is the essence of anarchism. Why are we against all imposed authority? Because we are *for* life. And life means diversity. As Kropotkin has said, "The condition of the maintenance of life is its expansion. . . ."

(Most continues, voice-under, as CAMERA CUTS

*to Fedya nudging Emma, who turns impatiently
away, intent on not missing any of Most's words.)*

MOST *(voice-over)*:   . . . Everywhere false imper-
atives, dishonest taboos. Anarchism demands
that the cycle end. Anarchism insists that to
become human we must scorn to rule and refuse
to be ruled. And *that* is why socialism is wrong-
headed. It puts faith in political action and in
the state as the vehicle for social transfor-
mation. . . .

*(Fedya persists in getting Emma's attention, point-
ing to a man several rows away. Emma shakes her
head no, she doesn't recognize him. CLOSE-UP on
Fedya long enough to hear him say:)*

FEDYA: Vladimir Heins . . . Russian nobleman . . .
heads a Christian communist colony . . . self-re-
generation through self-discipline . . . no *meat*—
no *steak*!

*(Emma laughs in mock contrition, then hushes
Fedya so she can listen to Most. CLOSE-UP of Most
as he finishes his speech.)*

MOST: . . . but surely we have learned by now
that parliaments are mere Houses of Mario-
nettes. And surely we have learned, too, that
means become ends. If you use the state to ob-
tain your goal, the state becomes your goal . . .
an end unto itself.

*(CUT TO: A section of the audience, cheering and
waving the black flag of anarchism.)*

(CUT TO: Emma, who in her excitement, leans over

and impulsively hugs Berkman. He is startled,
annoyed.)

(CUT TO: Schleier, now in the speaker's position.)

SCHLEIER: You talk of means becoming ends. A commendable warning. Yet it seems a curious one coming from Johann Most, the man who wrote *Science of Revolutionary Warfare*—a manual for preparing nitroglycerin bombs.

(CUT TO: Berkman's face, eyes glistening. Some in the audience are applauding, others booing and shouting for Schleier to sit down.)

SCHLEIER: The "propaganda of the deed," as you call it. In other words, Dr. Most, you advocate the use of violence to bring about a nonviolent society. Are anarchists a separate breed of men, able to use any means without becoming contaminated by them?

(Most strides angrily to the podium.)

MOST: I will take exactly one minute to clarify. Though with a mind as muddled as yours, sir, I doubt it will be time well spent. I have advocated "propaganda by the deed" *only* when other avenues to change have been foreclosed. Even the Nazarene, who came to preach peace, resorted to violence to drive the money changers from the temple.

(CUT TO: Fedya, shaking his head in disapproval. Berkman applauding wildly. Emma, uncertainly, starts applauding, too.)

MOST: No group in power has ever surrendered

it voluntarily. In every case the use of force—or the threat of it—is required. How can socialists claim that they abhor violence when they defend government—for the state is the chief promoter of violence. Or have you not heard of something called war? If you kill the state's enemies, you are a hero. But if you use violence *against* the state, you are a murderer. Anarchists do not believe that there is "good" violence and "bad" violence. We despise *all* violence, all coercion. But before we can create a society free of coercion, those in control of the state—the state itself—must be dislodged. And sometimes by violence.

(Pandemonium in the auditorium.)

MAN: Romantic!

ANOTHER MAN: Utopianism!

(CUT TO: A man jumping to his feet.)

MAN *(shouting at Most):*   You speak like a fool! Man is by nature an aggressive animal. Remove the restraints of government, and you will have chaos, not harmony.

VOICE: Bourgeois ideology!

MAN: Socialism is based on the hard facts of life. Socialism is realism. Anarchism is utopianism.

(CUT TO: Emma, rising almost involuntarily from her seat. She begins to speak.)

EMMA: The *height* of "realism" is to recognize that what does not yet exist, what has never been tried, is nonetheless possible! The *true* realist is he who rejects so-called "historical necessity" in the name of what is not yet known.

(Tremendous applause. Emma dazed, as if awakening from a trance. She suddenly becomes self-conscious, fumbling. Berkman helps her to her seat.)

(JUMP CUT TO: Crowd gathering around Emma to congratulate her. Most comes up.)

MOST: And who is this remarkable young lady?

EMMA: Dr. Most, I apologize. I didn't mean to—

MOST: Apologize? You spoke eloquently. Don't you agree, Berkman?

BERKMAN: Louise Michel come to life.

EMMA: Who?

MOST: *Who?* The heroine of the Paris Commune! Apparently your gifts are natural, not studied.

EMMA: I haven't read as much as I should.

FEDYA: Except for Chernyshevsky.

MOST: You must read more. The Germans. The revolutionary poets: Freiligrath, Schiller, Heine. I will prepare a list for you. But I still do not know your name.

EMMA: Emma Goldman. And this is my sister, Helena.

MOST: There are few women in our ranks. They come to meetings to find men. Then both vanish, like the fishermen at the lure of the Lorelei. The revolutionary zeal of womanhood has never impressed me.

BERKMAN: Emma is from Russia.

MOST *(sardonic)*: Ah yes, passionate Russia. We shall see. *(to Emma)* You have talent as a speaker. Notable talent. It must be put to use.

EMMA: But I've never spoken in public before. I didn't know what I was doing.

BERKMAN: No false modesty, Emma. With comrades, it only wastes time.

MOST: Tomorrow we'll talk more. I must go to the newspaper. No one else, it seems, can write a line of copy. Where are you staying, Miss Goldman?

EMMA: Well, Helena and I are—

FEDYA: —She's staying with us.

(CUT TO: Emma's astonished face.)

FEDYA: Why not? Comrades share, remember? We have a whole loft, and no one but me, Sasha, and—when we aren't fighting—Anya.

MOST: Come for me at *Die Freiheit* tomorrow night, Miss Goldman. I'll take you to Terrace Garden, and we will talk more of Louise Michel.

EMMA: Thank you, Dr. Most.

MOST: Let us say nine o'clock. Good evening, everyone. (*Most exits.*)

HELENA: Emma, how marvelous!

EMMA: I can't believe it!

BERKMAN: You must be careful, Emma. Most is attracted to you.

EMMA: Sasha—he could be my father! And what could he see in me, a factory girl, uneducated.

BERKMAN: Revolutionaries have no right to a personal life.

FEDYA *(to Berkman):* Who would believe it—*you* criticizing Johann Most, chief theoretician of "the deed"!

BERKMAN *(gruff):* It's time to go home.

FEDYA: Come along, Emma. You too, Helena.

HELENA: No, no, I'll stay with Aunt. I'm the family conservative.

EMMA: I don't know, Fedya, do you think—

FEDYA: Think? Think what? Are you going to give us another speech—this one on bourgeois morality?

EMMA: Sasha: Do *you* invite me?

BERKMAN: You've been invited.

FEDYA: Be a little more cordial, dear comrade.

BERKMAN *(suppressed fury)*: I warn you, Fedya, don't toy with me. I am not, like you, a part-time revolutionist. My life is for the Cause. Yes, Emma can stay with us. Because she cares about our principles.

FEDYA *(sarcastic)*: It's the Cause I was thinking of. Offering a haven in this hard city to Dr. Most's promising lecturer.

BERKMAN: And there will be no more talk of Most.

(Berkman storms ahead. As Emma and Helena embrace—FADE OUT.)

(FADE IN: The Buford (scene one). Emma is being shaken awake by a guard.)

GUARD: Hey! Hey!!

EMMA: What . . . what is it?

GUARD: Are you alive or dead?

EMMA: Is something wrong? Has something happened to Sasha?

GUARD: Who the hell is Sasha?

EMMA *(sitting upright)*: Who the hell are *you*?

GUARD: A private in the United States Army. I have my orders about you.

EMMA: Is one of them to prevent me from sleeping?

GUARD: You've been asleep twelve hours.

EMMA: *What?* I've never slept that long in my life.

GUARD: It must be because you can smell Russia ahead.

EMMA: It must be because the United States Army kept us awake for three days.

(Emma gets out of bed and heads toward the cabin door.)

GUARD: Where do you think you're going?

EMMA: To the toilet. Any objection?

GUARD: You don't go without me.

EMMA: Fine. I'm always glad for new experiences— and the chance to share them.

(CAMERA PANS to the guard's confused face.)

(DISSOLVE TO: Door leading into Terrace Garden. Most and Emma are seated at a table in animated conversation. CLOSE-UP—the bottle of wine Most holds in his hand. The label reads "Liebfrauen-milch.")

EMMA: What a lovely name—"milk of woman's love."

MOST: For wine, yes. For woman's love, no. The one is always poetry. The other finally prose.

EMMA: I've never tasted wine. Father wouldn't allow it.

MOST: And have you tasted love? Or did Father forbid that, too.

EMMA: I learned not to listen to Father.

(Most laughs, then raises his wine glass in a toast.)

MOST: *Prosit,* my young, naive lady!

EMMA *(bristling):* We mature early in my family.

MOST *(roars with laughter):* Very well! To my mature, ardent comrade! *(they drink.)* There is great need in our ranks for ardent ones. And I have great need for ardent friendship.

EMMA: You're idolized by thousands.

MOST: Yes, *mein Kind,* idolized, but not loved. One can be very lonely among thousands. Did you know that?

(CLOSE-UP—Emma's face. She is embarrassed.)

MOST: Where did you get silky blond hair and blue eyes? You said you were Jewish.

EMMA: At the pigs' market, my father would say.

(Most laughs again.)

MOST: I haven't had such a happy evening in years. You have a ready tongue, my little girl.

EMMA: Please don't call me that. I'm a young woman, not a child.

MOST: Indeed you are a woman, Emma. May I call you that?

EMMA: Yes, I'd like you to.

MOST: Good. And you are to call me Johann. Now, Emma. Do you know what I have in mind for you?

EMMA *(downcast)*:   Lecturing.

MOST *(impatient)*:   Yes, lecturing—but later, later. After you've read more and I've explained the social struggle to you, the mistakes of Marx, the glories of Bakunin. But now, Emma, what I have in mind for you *now*—is music and theater. *Carmen* at the Metropolitan, the plays of Schiller at the Yiddish Art!

(Emma almost jumps with excitement.)

EMMA: Oh, Johann, I once saw an opera. When I was ten in Königsberg, my teacher took me to *Trovatore*. How I cried! *(gestures in flamboyant self-parody)* "Ach, ich vergehe und sterbe hier! O, teuere Mutter, O teuere Mutter."

(They both break into gales of laughter.)

MOST: You're born for the stage, my little *Blondkopf*. You must see *all* of Schiller: *Wilhelm Tell, Die Raüber, Fiesco*, all. *(whispering in a confiding voice)* Did anyone ever tell you that Johann Most, the dangerous anarchist, wanted more than anything in this world to be an actor? It was my passion as a young man, my obsession. I saved every pfennig to buy tickets. And always for Schiller. Above all, I longed to perform Schiller. Aah . . .

EMMA: Then you should have, Johann. Everyone should do what he wants to do.

MOST: I did try once. The theater manager told me I might make a clown, but never an actor . . . well, you know . . . my face . . . Not exactly a matinee idol . . .

(Emma, touched, puts her hand on Most's sleeve.)

MOST *(animated)*:   You may not believe it, Emma, but I was a handsome youth. *(he touches his cheek)* Then some strange poisoning here. And a bad surgeon. *(laughs)*

(In the background the band starts to play Strauss.)

MOST: Ah—*Der Zigeunerbaron!*

EMMA: Oh, let's dance, Johann! Can we dance?

MOST: I think I can remember how.

(They move to the dance floor. As they pass one table, Most acknowledges two young men and briefly introduces Emma. Most and Emma start to dance. He is awkward, stiff; Emma is unembarrassed, increasingly reckless.)

(CUT TO: The two young men, whispering disapprovingly to each other. One rises and motions to Most. He and the young man start to confer. Emma slows down, then stops. She joins the conversation, which rapidly becomes heated, the words at first indistinguishable. Emma starts gesturing angrily.)

YOUNG MAN: It's undignified, frivolous. It hurts the Cause.

EMMA: I do what I want—that *is* the Cause!

MOST: Be calm, Emma.

YOUNG MAN: People are watching.

EMMA: They're watching because you interfered. Anarchists are supposed to mind their own business—and only their own.

YOUNG MAN: We can discuss it another time.

EMMA *(raising her voice)*: I haven't joined the movement to become a nun. The movement isn't a cloister.

(The band stops playing.)

EMMA: If I can't dance, it isn't my revolution!

MOST *(embarrassed)*: Come, Emma.

(He starts to lead her away. She yells back at the young man.)

EMMA: Anarchism is freedom from convention.

YOUNG MAN: Theatrics! Egotism!

(As Emma leans down to take off her shoe to throw, DISSOLVE TO: SHOT of shoe hitting against the wall. We are in the loft apartment. Emma is screaming at Berkman. Fedya and Anya can be seen disappearing into another room.)

EMMA: I will *not* be told what I must do and when I must do it! Not by you, not by anyone!

BERKMAN: Most has no right to squander money. We'd all like to eat and drink at Terrace Garden. You have to decide what you care about.

EMMA: I care about many things.

BERKMAN *(acidly)*: Precisely. You lack priorities. For you pleasure and revolution are coequal.

EMMA: I became an anarchist to assert my humanity, not to deny it.

BERKMAN: Sentimentality. You're a child. You understand nothing.

EMMA: I understand the difference between sentiment and emotion.

BERKMAN *(almost to himself)*: Precisely what I said about Edelstadt.

EMMA: I can't hear you!

BERKMAN: *Edelstadt*! An anarchist. A poet. I shared a room with him. He died two years ago of tuberculosis.

EMMA: What does that have to do with—

BERKMAN *(interrupting; furious)*: They wanted to take money from the treasury to send him to Denver. I refused to agree. *(he starts to crumble)* No funds belonging to the movement should ever be spent for private purposes. Most must be held

to account. Revolutionary ethics demand that . . .
(*starts to sob*) he died . . . I shared a room with
him. . . .

(*Emma rushes to comfort him.*)

EMMA: Oh, Sasha, how terrible! Sasha . . .
Sasha . . .

(*She tries to embrace him, but he moves away—
gently.*)

BERKMAN (*quietly*):   I don't matter. No individual
matters.

EMMA: Sasha, you're either a knave or a hero.

BERKMAN: I'm an instrument. Nothing more.

EMMA: Instruments don't have feelings.

BERKMAN: I've learned to control my feelings.

EMMA: Have you ever been in love, Sasha?

BERKMAN: Yes.

EMMA: What happened?

BERKMAN: She wanted to marry.

EMMA: How foolish of her.

(*CLOSE-UP—Berkman, surprised.*)

EMMA: I've been married.

BERKMAN: That can't be.

EMMA (*amused*):   It's very easy to get married, Sasha. Many people manage it.

BERKMAN: But you're so young.

EMMA: He worked the machine next to mine in Garson's factory. He talked well and read a lot. Father had always said (*laughs*) "You have too much energy, you'll become a whore." So I married. It lasted less than a year. He was impotent. I made the mistake of being sympathetic. That drove him to gambling. So I left.

BERKMAN: Did you mind he couldn't be your lover?

EMMA: Of course I minded. Wouldn't you?

BERKMAN: Have you ever been with a man?

EMMA: A boy I knew in St. Petersburg worked in one of the great hotels. He took me one day to see the rooms. In one of them, he seized me and tore open my waist dress.

BERKMAN: How awful.

EMMA: I was as eager as he. The only shock was to find out how wild contact can be between a man and a woman.

BERKMAN: Shameful.

EMMA (*laughs*):   It was a beautiful room. And he was handsome. But marriage?—never again. If I love a man, I'll give myself to him without rabbis and laws. And when the love passes, I'll leave without permission. (*pause*) Sasha . . . are you attracted to me?

BERKMAN: Of course.

EMMA: I'm glad. I feel the same.

(She moves toward him and affectionately puts her arms around him. He moves away.)

BERKMAN: Emma, I beg you. I cannot risk personal attachments.

EMMA: I want no *attachment*. I give freely and take freely. Different people call out different qualities in me.

BERKMAN: You mean you'd let several men share you?

EMMA *(angry)*:   What a stupid word!

BERKMAN *(abstractedly)*:   Everyone is free to do what they want.

EMMA: How would you feel if I gave myself to Johann?

BERKMAN *(trying to conceal his upset)*:   I just said, everyone is a free agent. If you're attracted to him, sleep with him.

EMMA: I'm not physically attracted. But he needs affection. He gives so much to others.

BERKMAN *(sardonic)*:   Duty calls, eh?

EMMA: I respond to Johann. To his sadness, his tenderness.

BERKMAN: That's not what I call love.

EMMA: I didn't call it anything.

BERKMAN: You can't sleep with a man who doesn't arouse you.

EMMA: I just told you he *did*.

BERKMAN: I mean physically.

EMMA: That's *your* idea of love.

BERKMAN *(angry)*:   You talk gibberish. The physical is everything to you, it's nothing to you! You sleep with a young boy because you want him, with an old man because he wants you!

EMMA *(cool)*:   You care too much about logic.

BERKMAN: I like to make sense out of life!

EMMA: You like to put sense into it.

(Berkman starts pacing, increasingly angry.)

BERKMAN: Do you intend to sleep with Most? Answer me directly!

EMMA: I don't plan my feelings.

BERKMAN: You'd better plan! You can be sure Most has plans. He's out to seduce you—you fool!

EMMA: He doesn't have to seduce me. All he has to do is tell me his honest feelings, so I can respond to them. And he does. He doesn't disguise his feelings behind theories.

(Berkman explodes. He jumps on Emma and starts

tearing at her clothes. They grapple on the couch. He rips her dress, then starts kissing her passionately. He repeats over and over:)

BERKMAN: *Dorogaya . . . dorogaya . . .*

(As they embrace, DISSOLVE TO: Most's office at Die Freiheit. He and Emma are consulting a large map of New York State.)

MOST: Binghamton will be the best place for you to try your wings. There's an active group of comrades in the city. You'll have a friendly audience. After that, Plattsburgh, Oswego, Syracuse, Utica—

EMMA: Johann, do you *really* think I can? I'm frightened to death. I don't even know what to talk about.

MOST: Stop being foolish. We've been over it many times. Above all, you're to argue against the movement for an eight-hour day, to say that it will dilute discontent. The workers must be made to see that our aim is to destroy capitalism, not reform it.

EMMA: But will they listen to a woman?

MOST: They will listen to Emma Goldman. If I can't resist her, how can they? *(embraces her)* You have reawakened me to life, Emma. I thought . . . all "this" was over for me. But my *Blondkopf* has made me young again. You will be my helpmate, my voice. I want you for my own.

(CLOSE-UP—Emma's face, tensing at the last re-

mark. The tension in her face dissolves into laugh-
ter. As CAMERA PULLS BACK we see that Emma is
naked from the waist up. She is posing for Fedya.)

EMMA: Fedya, my back is killing me. I agreed to
pose, but not for the entire day.

FEDYA: I can't concentrate.

EMMA: You should paint roses. They're less erotic.

FEDYA: . You're a shameless woman.

EMMA: I'm a tired woman. (*starts to get up*) And I
still have to pack. The train is in two hours.

(Emma starts to get dressed.)

EMMA: Fedya, I'm so excited. I can't believe this is
happening to me.

(Fedya comes toward her.)

FEDYA: You have a marvelous body, Emma. It's of
the earth.

EMMA: It's a peasant's body. Artists are supposed
to like delicate things.

FEDYA: Then maybe I'm not an artist.

(He retreats to the sofa. Emma continues to dress.)

EMMA: Helena will come with me as far as Rochester. She'll probably remain there with our
other sister, Lena. They say work is easier to get
in Rochester. Lena even talks of saving enough

to bring over our parents. I don't know what to think of that. Helena's had a letter that Father was near death after a throat operation. "He should have died long ago," I told her. She says I must be more forgiving, his harshness to me was only the frustration of his life, a man who never had a chance to use the energy of—

(She stops in midsentence as she catches sight of Fedya, his head buried in the pillow, sobbing.)

EMMA: Fedya—my God, what's wrong!

(She rushes over to him and puts her arm around him.)

EMMA: Fedya, what is it, what is it?

FEDYA: I've tried to fight it, Emma, because of Sasha. I know how much he loves you.

EMMA: And I love Sasha. Fiercely—as Sasha is fierce. But what is that to do with us? Do you think my emotions are so puny that they are drained by a single expression. (*laughs*) Only the bourgeois think you must love one person at a time.

FEDYA *(confused)*:   But . . . but the physical part . . . the . . .

EMMA: If feeling is there, the rest follows. There are many kinds of feeling, and there are many ways of expressing it. There is no conflict, only wider fulfillment.

FEDYA: Sasha would be wild. He would never share you.

(Emma's face clouds with anger.)

EMMA: You, Sasha, Johann—you all use the same words! The words of possession. No one possesses me, and so no one "shares" me. I respond to what someone calls out. And if any of you try to restrict my response, then you'll call out nothing. Besides, you're wrong about Sasha. He believes in freedom. In any case, there'll be no deception.

FEDYA *(quietly)*:   Emma, you're a marvel.

(She leans down and embraces him. DISSOLVE TO: CLOSE-UP—Emma's and Berkman's faces. Intimate, intense, soft.

BERKMAN: I believe in your freedom to love. Yes, I'm jealous. It's part of my background. I hate it. And I'll conquer it. The jealousy would be worse if Fedya wasn't my friend and comrade. And if I thought of you merely as a woman. But you're more than that to me. You're a fighter and a revolutionary.

EMMA: Sasha, you're more beautiful than I even knew. We're two sane romantics in a crazy world.

(They embrace)

BERKMAN: Now hurry! Or Binghamton will never see our new Perovskaya!

(CAMERA PULLS BACK to reveal that Berkman and Emma are standing near a train. In the background are Fedya and Most. The latter is frowning and fidgeting. Emma and Berkman embrace

again, then she runs for the train. She stands on the last step of the platform as the train pulls out. Berkman rushes up.)

BERKMAN: I almost forgot. *(hands her an American Beauty rose)* As a token of my love, *Dushenka*. And a harbinger of luck!

FEDYA *(warmly teasing)*:   Such extravagance!

(Berkman laughs. The two men embrace, and stand with their arms around each other waving good-bye to Emma. She is crying as the train pulls out. Most stands apart—physically and emotionally. He calls after Emma as the train pulls away.)

MOST: Remember, Emma, you are my voice!

(CLOSE-UP—Emma's face. A shadow of displeasure crosses it. FREEZE.)

(DISSOLVE TO: Emma's face. She is on the lecture platform.)

(CUT TO: The audience, which has only a handful of people in it. One of them is Helena.)

EMMA: . . . Anarchism is the philosophy of the sovereign individual. It is also a theory of social harmony. There is a mistaken notion that anarchism means destruction and chaos, that it encourages individual freedom at the expense of social cohesion. That is a false image spread by the enemies of anarchism in order to pervert its message. . . .

(CUT TO: The audience, bored. CUT TO: Helena, upset that Emma's abstractions are losing the audience's attention.)

EMMA: There is no conflict between the individual and the social instinct, any more than there is between the heart and the lungs. Anarchism is against the organization of the state because the state represents dictation from above, putting the needs of the powerful few in place of the needs of the multitude. Anarchism asserts the possibility of *voluntary* association to fulfill the *actual* needs of those involved. It means a new kind of social organism. Our opponents say that our ideal is impractical. But as Oscar Wilde has said, a practical scheme, to the conservative mind, means one that is either already in existence, or one that could be carried out only under existing conditions.

(Tepid applause from audience. Emma retreats in confusion from the stage. DISSOLVE TO: Emma and Helena.)

HELENA: I know it's all true and important. But I kept thinking: "Where's *Emma* in what she's saying?"

EMMA: I'm not separate from my ideas.

HELENA: But you're more than your ideas. Talk about *your* life, about being a woman. The way you did to Papa.

EMMA: You used to beg me *not* to speak my mind to Papa.

HELENA: Then I was frightened for you. *(laughs)* Now I'm frightened for them!

EMMA: Johann wants me to concentrate on the eight-hour-day question.

HELENA: One papa is enough in every woman's life.

EMMA: Helena, you're becoming an emancipé!

HELENA: It's how I summon up courage to say good-bye.

(They embrace.)

EMMA: It won't be long, dear sister.

HELENA: Remember: *your own life*. You're one of the few capable of *living*. Now *tell* of it!

(CUT TO: Emma, on the platform.)

EMMA: For women, the home is prison and marriage a curse. I talk to you from my own experience. I have been a body slave in marriage, and a wage slave in capitalism. *(murmurs and boos from the audience)* The two institutions are alike: paternal and parasitic. Capitalism robs man of his birthright, stunts his growth, poisons his body, keeps him in ignorance and poverty. Marriage robs woman of independence, annihilates her social consciousness, paralyzes her imagination. *(louder boos)* Women are now calling for the vote. And the vote they must have. But true emancipation goes far beyond the vote. The most vital right is the right to love and be loved. And love is not compatible with subordination. A true conception of the relation of the sexes will not admit of conqueror and conquered; it knows of but one great thing: to give of one's self boundlessly, in order to find one's self richer, deeper, better. That alone can fill the emptiness. . . .

(Catcalls. Some of the audience stomp out in indig-nation. CUT TO: A man in the audience jumping to his feet.)

MAN: We came here, madam, to hear a discussion of the Social Question, not a panegyric to free love.

EMMA: My point, sir, is that women are part of society—or should be. We are tired of being treated as angels or whores. We want to be treated as human beings, to be placed on *earth.* When woman has learned to be as self-centered and as determined as man is, to delve into life as he does *and* pay the price for it, she will achieve her liberation. *And,* incidentally, will also help *him* become free.

(A second man rises in the audience.)

SECOND MAN: Your ideas would result in houses of prostitution at every street corner.

EMMA: Love given freely empties the houses of prostitution. Besides, sir, if the men of the future look like you, the houses will be emptier still.

(Laughter from the audience.)

THIRD MAN: I too advocate the same standards of behavior for women and for men. But unlike you, I advocate self-control not self-indulgence. I am forty years old, madam, and I am proud to say publicly that I have remained pure.

EMMA: Sir, I would advise a medical examination.

(As audience breaks into an uproar:)

(DISSOLVE TO: Emma's hotel room. She's asleep. A quiet, but persistent, tapping at her door. It finally wakes her. Without turning on a light, she gets out of bed and goes to the door.)

EMMA: Who is it?

MALE *(voice over):*   An admirer.

EMMA: What are you talking about? Who is it?

MALE: Please let me in. I heard you speak tonight at the Free Thought Society.

EMMA: It's the middle of the night. What do you want?

MALE: I'm a kindred spirit.

EMMA: I don't like spirits, kindred or otherwise. Go away.

MALE: Please, you don't understand. I agree with everything you said tonight. I am for freedom.

EMMA: I am for sleep! If you don't go away this minute, I'll start to scream. I'll scream so loud I'll wake the whole hotel.

MALE: No, no, please, I beg you! I'm a married man, with grown children. I'll go, I'll go. I thought you believed in free love.

EMMA: You're wrong—I charge one hundred dollars!

*(Sounds of the man hurrying off. CLOSE-UP—
Emma, shaking her head in mingled dismay and
amusement. She goes back to bed. She falls off into
a fitful doze. FADE OUT.)*

*(FADE IN: Emma's dream. Her father is hitting her
with his fist.)*

FATHER: You are my disgrace! You will always be
my disgrace! A loose woman! A whore!

*(Helena grabs her father and wrestles him away
from Emma. He becomes dizzy, falls headlong onto
the floor in a dead faint. Helena screams for her
mother. Emma raises her head from the floor.)*

EMMA *(screaming between her tears)*:   That's the
last time you'll ever do that. The *last*!

*(FREEZE on Emma's face. When it reanimates,
she's back on the lecture platform, in midspeech.
The audience is larger than before.)*

EMMA: . . . We have as much liberty as we are
willing to take. The wealthy few will go on rob-
bing you unless you become daring enough to
demand your rights. Demonstrate before the
palaces of the rich: Demand work. If they do not
give you work, demand bread. If they deny you
both, *take* bread. It is your sacred right!

*(Uproarious applause. Furious booing. An old man
rises in the audience. He is haggard and lean.)*

OLD MAN *(kindly)*:   If I may say a word or two, my
dear young lady.

EMMA: Of course. This is an open forum.

OLD MAN: I understand your impatience with capitalism. I can even remember my own. I like your new world, young lady. I think the anarchist dream is the best dream. But what are we old ones to do? We won't live to see the new world. Is it so wrong for us to try to get a few reforms, instead of holding out for the Revolution? All I can hope to see in my lifetime is an eight hour day. A few extra hours, maybe, for reading, or to walk in a park. Am I so wrong to want a little release?

(Applause from the audience. CLOSE-UP—Emma's face, upset at the poignancy of the man's words.)

EMMA *(fumbling)*: I . . . I meant only that . . . that the movement for an eight-hour day must not sidetrack our revolutionary energies. But I . . . I do understand what you say. . . . I sympathize with what you say. . . .

(A well-dressed man jumps up.)

MAN: Let us be clear what this woman has been advocating. She is for the appropriation of property. And for violence against those who wield authority. She is an extremist, a maniac.

EMMA: I do *not* advocate indiscriminate violence. The only potentates I would kill by any and all means at my disposal are—ignorance, superstition, and bigotry.

MAN: Do you or do you not advocate violence?

EMMA: Do you, sir, believe in government?

MAN: Of course. It is the basis of civilization.

EMMA: Government is the chief instrument of violence. Government is the criminal that hanged the Haymarket anarchists, that put to death five innocent men who had committed no crime other than to speak their minds. I quote to you, sir, what one of those anarchists, Louis Lingg, said after the state sentenced him to death: "Our silence will speak louder than the voices you strangle today. . . . We die confident that the thousands to whom we spoke will remember our words. And when you shall hang us, then, *they* will do the bomb throwing."

(FREEZE. DISSOLVE TO: Most's office. He's glaring at the headlines of various newspapers lying on his desk. ZOOM to the headlines:

FEMALE ANARCHIST ADVOCATES BOMB-THROWING

EMMA GOLDMAN SHOCKS AUDIENCE WITH DEFENSE OF FREE LOVE

TERRORIST WANTS TO DESTROY SOCIETY

Most slaps the newspapers angrily, then turns to Emma.)

MOST: This is not *my* voice!

EMMA: I discovered one of my own. And I must speak with it if I am to be heard.

MOST: Yes, yes, I know all about the poor old worker who brought you to tears. It's fine to feel sorry for old men—but their needs can't displace the needs of the future.

EMMA: Why can we not work on both fronts: for a long-range anarchist society and for the short-term amelioration of the workers' condition?

MOST *(laughs sardonically)*:   Mmm—so said the Social Democrats in Germany. Remember, my dear, that I once sat in the Reichstag. I know all about "legislation to help the workers." It *doesn't* help them. It buys them off. It loosens one shackle so that the rest of the chain can grip them more firmly. And in the process the masses come to believe that their rulers *care*. Make no mistake: It's the average man's faith in the existing order that constitutes the greatest obstacle to revolutionary change. And *that* is what you are encouraging.

EMMA *(upset)*:   I can't be a parrot. I have to say what I feel.

MOST: Like most of the young, you confuse feeling with thought. If you knew more, you would *feel* differently. *(slaps the newspapers again)* This is not your voice. It's Berkman's! That arrogant Russian Jew—what does he know of life?!

EMMA *(furious)*:   *I* am a Russian Jew! Is that a crime?!

MOST *(shifting to conciliatory tone)*:   *Liebschen, liebschen*, you have the opportunity to be a great woman, a leader. If only you would allow yourself to be guided. You know how much I need you, how much I care about you. I must get you to see that you cannot serve two causes at once. Or two men.

EMMA *(wrenching away from him)*:   I *serve* no one!

MOST *(getting angry again)*:   You're either for me or against me. You must *choose*.

EMMA: Sasha's very words. You two are more alike than either of you knows. The voice will be *my* voice—not yours, not Sasha's.

(She starts to leave. Most tries to grab hold of her, but she pulls free and walks out. ZOOM to Most's face, twisted with resentment and rage.)

(CUT TO: The loft apartment. Emma is at work at her sewing machine. Anya is stitching a dress.)

ANYA: If that's how you and Fedya feel, that's how you feel. At least you told me.

EMMA: Fedya agreed we should. There should be no secrets. And no hurt.

ANYA: Don't be foolish, Emma. There is hurt. You always want the best of all worlds.

EMMA: I want the best for all of us.

ANYA: Too bad Sasha and I aren't attracted to each other. That might help.

(Berkman enters, dejected.)

EMMA: No luck, eh?

BERKMAN: Nothing. They're even laying off the day laborers. I've never seen so many out of work.

(Emma holds up the coat she's sewing.)

EMMA: We're all right, Sashenka. Mrs. Korngold's promised me ten dollars for it. And I'll have it done by tomorrow.

(Berkman slumps onto the sofa.)

BERKMAN: I've been out of work too long. It's bad for a man.

EMMA *(resentfully)*:   It's bad for anyone.

(Fedya comes bursting into the room.)

FEDYA: There's been a pitched battle at Homestead between the strikers at U.S. Steel and the Pinkertons! Half a dozen workers have been killed! Frick has gotten the governor to declare martial law!

(The others rush over to him.)

EMMA AND ANYA: Fedya—*what?* When did it happen? How many killed?

FEDYA: Last night. Frick hired Pinkerton detectives to break the strike. They attacked last night. The workers had been tipped off. They fought them off twice, then set fire to oil slick all around the river. The Pinkertons threw down their arms—they *surrendered!*

(Emma and Anya gasp with amazement. They dance a jig around the room. Berkman is deathly quiet. CLOSE-UP shows the intensity in his eyes.)

EMMA: The workers are awake! Awake!

FEDYA: A little boy was among those killed. Dozens are wounded.

BERKMAN: The waiting is over. At last.

FEDYA: Frick still refuses any negotiations. He says he's dealing with a riot, not a strike, that the anarchists are responsible. He vows to crush them. It's a declaration of war.

(Berkman grabs his jacket and starts to leave.)

EMMA: Sasha—where are you going?

BERKMAN: I must see Most.

EMMA: *Most? Why Most?*

BERKMAN: The moment has come. The right moment has finally come.

(Berkman exits. BLACKOUT; FREEZE. The blackness begins to move. The CAMERA PANS the darkened apartment. PAN to Fedya and Anya curled up in bed, asleep in each other's arms. PAN to the bed shared by Emma and Berkman. Emma is alone, tossing in her sleep. Suddenly she wakes up, feels for Berkman, then jumps out of bed. She walks through the dark apartment looking for him, sees a light in the back room and follows it.)

(CUT TO: Berkman, his back to Emma as she approaches. He's absorbed in putting together the pieces of a mechanism spread out on the floor. Emma calls to him softly.)

EMMA: Sasha . . .

(He jumps.)

BERKMAN *(angry whisper):*   Dammit . . . Go back to bed.

EMMA: What is all this?

BERKMAN: You'll wake the others. I'll tell you in time.

(CAMERA FOLLOWS Emma as she bends down to examine the pieces of metal. A book is open on the floor. The CAMERA catches its title: "Johann Most, Science of Revolutionary Warfare." She picks up the book.)

EMMA: The deed.

BERKMAN: The moment is right. Frick's death will echo around the world. Most agrees.

EMMA: Then let Most do it.

BERKMAN: It will strike terror into the hearts of exploiters everywhere. It will prove the working class has its avengers.

EMMA: Sasha, listen to me. Johann would like nothing better than to have you out of the way for good.

BERKMAN: The deed will give us possession of ourselves. It will make us men.

EMMA: *Sasha!*

BERKMAN *(as if coming out of a trance)*:   What?

EMMA: Let Most throw the bomb. Let him *build* it at least. *(throws the book down)* He's the expert.

BERKMAN: No one will take that honor from me.

EMMA: It could go off in the building. It could kill Fedya and Anya, the people in the other apartments. Some of them are children.

BERKMAN: You're not ready for revolution *in practice.* That's why I didn't tell you.

EMMA: Sasha, *please* listen to me. There are better ways to help the Homestead workers. Think of the families of those who have already been killed. We can start a fund-raising campaign for them. They're destitute. Frick has thrown some of them out of—

BERKMAN *(ice cold):*   —and we could send you on another speaking tour about the eight-hour day. I'm tired of words.

(Pause.)

EMMA: I'm going with you.

BERKMAN *(disconcerted):*   We can't spend two lives on one man.

EMMA: If I'm along, it will be easier to escape. A woman can—

BERKMAN: —I'm not interested in escaping. The time regulator on the bomb will let me save myself. But for one purpose only: so I can justify my act in court, so the American people can see I am neither insane nor criminal. The court will condemn me to death. But I'll die by my own hand. *You* must stay alive. You must plead the meaning of my deed to the world, make it see that my act was not directed against Frick the man, but Frick the symbol of injustice. We must each serve the Cause in the way we are best equipped. My job is to commit the deed. Yours is to explain it.

EMMA: No one decides what my "job" is. I'm going with you to Pittsburgh.

(FREEZE.)

(MONTAGE: Series of quick cuts.

Emma holding the light as Berkman works.

Emma pointing to sections of Most's manual to help Berkman solve a particular mechanical problem.

Emma tiptoeing around the apartment to check that Fedya and Anya are asleep.

Emma and Berkman, the bomb complete, carrying it with them wrapped in a satchel, on the Third Avenue Elevated.

A deserted field in New Jersey, flooded with moonlight.

Berkman prepares the fuse.

He and Emma take cover.

Emma puts her fingers in her ears, as she leans against Berkman's chest.

Seconds pass. Nothing happens. The bomb has failed to detonate.)

(CUT TO: The loft apartment. Berkman, Emma, Fedya, and Anya.)

BERKMAN: I wouldn't have told you, I wouldn't have involved you. But now I need help. The bomb used up all but fifteen dollars. It costs fourteen to get to Pittsburgh. I need a new suit to help me get into Frick's office. And a revolver to take the place of the bomb.

FEDYA: This is *not* Czarist Russia! There are other avenues to change besides assassination.

BERKMAN: It's worse than Russia. Just enough attention is paid to the workers' needs to blunt discontent, to make them indifferent to their own misery.

FEDYA: If they're indifferent, why shouldn't you be?

BERKMAN: Progress depends on a few. Only a few can see what is needed. They open the eyes of the others.

FEDYA: Now you think you're the Savior!

BERKMAN: If you won't help, say so.

FEDYA: The workers in America *crucify* their Christs!

EMMA: No, Fedya. The workers *will* understand. They know Frick and U.S. Steel are the enemy— and that's all they need to know.

FEDYA: Rubbish! You saw the telegram the strikers sent to Andrew Carnegie in Scotland: "Kind master, tell us what you wish us to do and we shall do it for you." Ugh! I tell you the workers will be the first to call you a murderer, not a savior. All you'll do is convince them that anarchism means violence—which is what our enemies have been telling them for years. You may kill Frick, but you'll kill anarchism along with him.

ANYA *(to Emma)*:   I gather you approve.

(CLOSE-UP on Emma, uneasy.)

EMMA: I'm going with Sasha.

FEDYA *(to Berkman, angrily)*:   You've talked her into it.

EMMA: No one talks me into anything.

ANYA: Not by arguing with you, maybe. By letting you love them.

EMMA: My political decisions are not a function of my glands.

BERKMAN *(quietly)*:   The matter has been decided for us. There simply isn't enough money for two people to get to Pittsburgh.

EMMA *(rising)*:   I will get enough money.

ANYA: Where are you going at this time of night?

EMMA: I will tell you all about it later.

(As she turns to leave the apartment, the CAMERA FREEZES on her back. When it pulls back, we see Emma standing nervously in a doorway. She has on cheap black stockings and high heels. She leaves the doorway and starts walking slowly

down the street. Two other girls, dressed in flashy clothes, eye Emma as they saunter by. One of them calls out.)

GIRL: A bad night, sweetie.

(Emma ducks into a doorway. To calm down, she massages her temples. CLOSE-UP—the motion of her hands against her forehead. The undulating lines wave and give way to Emma walking slowly across the living room of her father's house trying to balance a glass of water in her hand. The glass tips and crashes to the floor. Her father screams at her, and comes toward her across the room with his hand raised to strike her. As the blow is about to descend, a man's voice booms out at her in the doorway.)

MAN: Hey, lady, you in business or not?

(Emma looks up, startled, into the face of a fat, drunken man. She mumbles:)

EMMA: No . . . no . . .

(and darts out of the doorway, almost running down the street. At the corner she gets hold of herself, and retraces her steps back to the doorway. From a distance the CAMERA picks up a man of about sixty, white haired, tall, distinguished, watching Emma. As he moves toward her, she steels herself not to run.)

MAN *(gently)*:   Would you care to have a drink with me, miss?

(Emma nods yes. He offers his arm and they move

down the street. CUT TO: Emma and the man at a table in a saloon. Emma is trying to adjust her corset without being obvious.)

MAN: Looks like you're having a little trouble.

EMMA: I'm all right.

MAN: Have you ever worn a corset before?

EMMA: Of course. It's stuffy in here.

MAN: We can leave any time.

EMMA: I'd like another beer. My throat's parched.

(The man signals for more beer.)

MAN: You did a lot of walking.

(CLOSE-UP on Emma, surprised.)

MAN: I watched you going back and forth. You've got an interesting technique. Most of the girls slow down when a man approaches. You double your pace.

(Emma seems torn between laughter and tears. The man puts his hand understandingly on her arm.)

MAN: It's your first time, isn't it.

EMMA: Not . . . really.

MAN: You're not much of a liar, either.

EMMA: You have to go with me.

MAN *(amused)*:   Do I? How much are you offering?

EMMA: I *must* have fifteen dollars.

MAN: I'll tell you what. *(reaches in his billfold)* Here's ten, and we'll call it a night.

EMMA: You mean, you're going to just *give* me ten dollars?

MAN: Why not? That corset must have cost a pretty penny.

EMMA: I borrowed it.

MAN: I may be quite mistaken, but I've a feeling you're not cut out to be a streetwalker.

EMMA: No one is "cut out" to be a streetwalker. Thousands of young girls are driven by economic necessity, by the horrors of capitalist—

MAN: —now, now, none of that. Serious discussion bores me. You're an awfully nice kid, you know.

EMMA: I was twenty-three last month.

MAN: Mmm. There is something of the old lady about you. But even old folks can be silly. Look at me; I'm sixty-one and constantly doing foolish things. Now take your ten dollars and scoot home.

(As the man hands her the ten dollars, FREEZE. UNFREEZE as Emma hands it to Berkman.)

FEDYA *(laughing):* Well, who can blame him? Sex and a lecture on capitalism don't mix. Most is right: You were born for the platform.

(He and Anya laugh.)

BERKMAN *(angrily):* You're cheapening Emma's gesture. You're a shallow man.

EMMA: Yes, please, Fedya . . . it wasn't funny, not at all funny. . . . My father was . . . wrong . . . about me. . . .

(She starts to cry. Berkman puts his arms around her. FREEZE.)

(DISSOLVE OUT: Emma and Berkman on the sofa; his arm is still around her. Fedya and Anya are gone. It is almost dark.)

EMMA: But you're part of my flesh and blood. I can't just . . . go on. . . .

BERKMAN: You'll have to. What if I never have a trial? There'd be no one to tell the world of my purpose.

EMMA: Sasha, you can't be so hard.

BERKMAN: The task is hard. We must be.

EMMA: I'll never see you again.

BERKMAN: You'll be with me to the last. We must think of humanity.

EMMA: But isn't humanity . . . us?

(Berkman is silent.)

EMMA: What are you thinking about, dearest?

BERKMAN: In St. Petersburg, when I was ten, I heard the rabbinical saying that "with one instant of righteousness, the Messiah would come to earth." It seemed such a beautiful promise, so easy to fulfill. It preyed on my mind for weeks. How could I hasten the deliverance? Finally, I had the answer: At the stroke of noon on a given day, all the Jews in the world would bow down in prayer. That would be the instance of righteousness God required; the Messiah would come! I rushed to tell my Hebrew teacher about my plan. He smiled sadly. "No," he said, "the children of Israel couldn't be saved so easily. No man has the power," he told me, "to hasten the steps of the Deliverer. Necessity, necessity alone, with its iron heel, can wake the living dead." I was crushed at his words. Bitterly crushed. *(laughs grimly)* So what do you think of my Hebrew tutor and his parable?

EMMA: Parables always sound wise. And they always counsel submission.

(Berkman is pleased. He hugs Emma.)

BERKMAN: You do understand, dearest. We need a new hope. *(he kisses her gently and rises to go)* It's time.

EMMA: Oh no, Sasha . . . Sashenka . . . !

BERKMAN *(gently):* Shush . . . be still . . . *(he kisses her again, then moves away. Emma sits alone crying)*

EMMA: Sashenka . . . Sashenka . . .

(DISSOLVE TO: Reprise from scene one, dockside at the Buford:*)*

REPORTER: Mr. Berkman, do you find any irony in the fact that Henry Clay Frick . . . died this very week.

BERKMAN: Thousands of people have died this week.

REPORTER: Oh, come now, Mr. Berkman . . . Is that all you have to say about Frick?

BERKMAN: You can add: Mr. Frick has been deported by God.

(CUT TO: Receptionist's desk, Frick's outer office.)

BERKMAN: The name is Berkman, not Bergman.

(The receptionist starts to argue.)

RECEPTIONIST: As I told you yesterday, Mr. Berkman—

(The door to Frick's inner office opens. A servant comes out, hears the argument, walks over to the receptionist and picks up Berkman's calling card.)

SERVANT: Mister Frick is engaged. He cannot see you now, sir.

(He hands the card back to Berkman, who takes it and makes a feint toward leaving. Then he quickly turns about, pushes past the astonished reception-

ist and servant into Frick's office. Inside the office are Frick, his assistant, and a carpenter working on the bookshelves.)

BERKMAN: Which of you is Frick?

FRICK: I am Henry Clay Frick. And who are you, sir?

(CUT TO: CLOSE-UP—gun as Berkman takes it out of his pocket.)

BERKMAN: I'm here to avenge the Homestead workers you murdered.

(Berkman fires. Frick lets out a cry and falls. CUT TO: Berkman raising the gun to fire again. CUT TO: The assistant, leaping forward. He knocks the gun out of Berkman's hand. The two scuffle on the floor. The carpenter comes up behind Berkman with a hammer.)

FRICK: Murder! Help!

(The receptionist and servant rush in. Berkman gets hold of the gun again and fires a second time. The gun fails to go off. The carpenter hits him on the back of the head. Berkman manages, dazedly, to struggle free. He pulls a knife from his coat and plunges it into Frick's leg several times. Frick screams in pain. Shouting, stamping. The carpenter hits Berkman again. The others press down on him. He sinks into unconsciousness. Frick's voice comes through the din: "Don't kill him . . . the law . . . leave him to the law . . ." Repeat footage of Emma sitting on the sofa, crying softly, "Sasha . . . Sashenka . . .")

(CUT TO: Berkman, in his cell. He has his pants down. ZOOM to his hand, extracting a small ball of paper from his anus. ZOOM to the paper as Berkman unwraps it. Inside is a capsule. He puts it next to his cot, then lies back and begins to write a note.)

(CLOSE-UP—Writing pad. We read the words as Berkman writes them: "My darling Emma. Comrade, you were with me at the last. Tell them I gave up what was dearest to me for an ideal."

(SUPERIMPOSED OVER the pad: the image of Emma, Fedya, and Anya staring at newspaper headlines:

YOUNG MAN BY THE NAME OF ALEXANDER BERGMAN SHOOTS FRICK. ASSASSIN OVER-POWERED BY WORKING-MAN AFTER DESPERATE STRUGGLE.)

(CUT TO: Berkman's cell. Noise at his door. He grabs the capsule and tries to swallow it. But the guards rush in, pry his jaw open, and extract the capsule.)

GUARD *(examining the capsule):*   A dynamite cartridge.

(Shoves Berkman against the wall.)

GUARD: Thought you'd cheat the state, huh? *(shoves him again)* We got other plans for you. Murderers don't get off that easy.

BERKMAN: Unless they head up a government, or a corporation

(Guard hits Berkman so hard, he falls to the floor.)

CLOSE-UP—Berkman holding his bleeding head.

FREEZE. DISSOLVE OUT TO: Frick's head wrapped in bandages. He is in bed. It is piled high with newspapers, telegrams. ZOOM to several headlines:

FRICK OUT OF DANGER

PRESIDENT LAUDS FRICK COMPASSION TO ASSASSIN

STEELWORKERS UNION DENOUNCES ASSASSIN

(Frick is dictating a letter to his assistant.)

FRICK: With the strike broken and public sympathy on our side, we must use the occasion to maximum advantage. All workers associated with the union or the strike are to be fired immediately, and under no condition rehired. This is our chance, once and for all . . . to crush a union movement which for a time has threatened to—

(Secretary enters, holding out a telegram.)

SECRETARY: A telegram, Mr. Frick, from the president of the United States. He *will* be attending the testimonial in your honor.

FRICK *(as he reaches for the telegram)*:   How very gratifying.

(FREEZE. CUT TO: Sachs's Café. A meeting is in progress. The crowd is large and boisterous. Emma, Fedya, and Anya are seated in the middle of it; all three are holding hands. Most is speaking.)

MOST: . . . As I have said repeatedly in *Die Freiheit*, I have wanted time to think over the implications of Berkman's act before making any statement about it. I've chosen today, the day of Berkman's trial, to give my views. Indeed, before our meeting ends we should have news of the verdict. The staff at *Die Freiheit* is standing by the telegraph and will bring us word as soon as it arrives.

(CLOSE-UP on Emma, nervously clutching Fedya's hand. Anya puts her arm around Emma to soothe her.)

MOST: I note that the people closest to Berkman are with us today. Indeed, one of them, Miss Emma Goldman, has been implicated by several newspapers as an accomplice.

EMMA *(jumping to her feet)*: I cannot claim that honor for myself alone. The papers have also named you, Johann Most, as the one person, above all others, who has long urged the necessity of "the deed."

(Most tries to appear unperturbed, urbane.)

MOST: Quite right, Miss Goldman. The papers have mentioned my name. Often. And for that reason, too, it is necessary that I clarify my position today. That is, if Miss Goldman will allow me to continue.

(Emma is about to reply, but Fedya and Anya gently pull her back to her seat.)

(CUT TO: Berkman's trial. As he tries to read his statement, he is forcibly restrained, a gag pushed into his mouth. The judge delivers sentence, but the words cannot be heard. Berkman is half dragged from the court.)

(CUT TO: Sachs's Café.)

MOST: . . . When living in exile, in London, as you know, I publicly applauded the assassination of Czar Alexander II. For doing so, I was sentenced to eighteen months at hard labor. My friends advised me to flee. I refused. I served the sentence gladly.

(CLOSE-UP—Emma, somewhat relieved at Most's last words. Several people sitting near her give her reassuring pats.)

MOST: But, my friends, the United States is not Czarist Russia.

(Murmurs in the crowd. Emma starts to rise again, but Fedya restrains her.)

MOST: Each "deed" must be judged individually, on its merits. *(pause)* Which brings us to Alexander Berkman. *(pause)* Rumors have abounded that he was one of Frick's own agents.

(Shouts from the crowd:)

FIRST VOICE: Shame!

SECOND VOICE: Slander!

(Most raises his hands for quiet.)

MOST: I, for one, have never given the slightest credence to such reports—though it does seem strange that at such close range Berkman failed to kill Frick.

(Angry shouts from the crowd.)

MOST: I have since learned, however, that Berkman had little practice with a gun—other than target shooting at Russian picnics.

(Some in the crowd laugh, others boo. Emma jumps up again.)

EMMA: I warn you, Johann Most! I am here to defend Sasha's honor—even if that means destroying yours!

(CLOSE-UP—Most's face. A brief flicker of fear.)

MOST: Miss Goldman is hysterical. There's no point proceeding if she's to be allowed these outbursts.

(Most sits down abruptly. Contradictory shouts from the crowd:)

VOICE: Throw her out!

SECOND VOICE: Bring her to the front!

THIRD VOICE: Let her speak!

FOURTH VOICE: Get rid of her!

(CUT TO: The doorway. A man rushes into the room and makes his way toward Most. When he reaches him, he whispers in his ear. Most rises and raises his hands for quiet.)

MOST: Your attention! Your attention!

(The crowd quiets.)

MOST: We have word from Berkman's trial! Quiet, please! Word has arrived about Berkman!

(ZOOM to Emma, her face terror-stricken. Fedya grabs her, and with Anya they move to the front.)

MOST: Word has just come over the telegraph. The trial is over. The judge refused to let Berkman deliver his statement.

VOICE: The sentence! What was the sentence?!

MOST: Felonious assault is ordinarily punished by seven years in prison. Berkman has been sentenced to twenty-two years.

(Pandemonium in the crowd. ZOOM to Emma, near hysteria. She violently pushes Fedya and Anya away and starts toward Most.)

(CLOSE-UP—Emma's face. Tears pour down her cheeks. Her words are barely audible:)

EMMA: . . . a tomb . . . a tomb . . .

(She reaches Most.)

EMMA *(screaming)*: Traitor! Traitor! Frick lives. You live. And Sasha is in a tomb! You—our teacher, our father!

(CLOSE-UP—Emma's hand as it comes out from under her coat. A horse whip is in it.)

(ZOOM to Most's face, horrified as he catches sight of the whip. His hand almost involuntarily goes to his twisted jaw.)

(Before anyone can stop her, Emma lashes Most

across the face and neck with the whip, all the while screaming "Traitor!" at him. The whip breaks. Emma throws the pieces at Most, who lies crouched on the floor trying to protect his head.)

(Fedya reaches Emma and forcibly restrains her. She collapses in his arms.)

(FREEZE on Fedya's arm around Emma. UN-FREEZE: His arm is still around her. They are sitting on a park bench.)

FEDYA: I'll take you to friends. They can hide you for a few days. With your name in the papers, the police will be looking for you.

EMMA: No. I can't endanger anyone else. I'll be all right. I'll find a room.

FEDYA: You should leave New York for a while.

EMMA: I'll see.

FEDYA: At least Sasha is alive. We can work for his release. You must lead the protest. You can travel the country explaining Sasha's motives.

EMMA *(kissing him on the cheek)*:   You say all this even though you're against what he did.

FEDYA: Sasha isn't responsible.

EMMA *(startled)*:   Sasha knew exactly what he was doing! Don't take that from him. If he wasn't responsible, then who?

FEDYA: No one . . . things . . .

EMMA: Nonsense.

FEDYA: I suppose you knew what you were doing when you attacked Most?

EMMA: *(uncertain)*:   Of course. I knew I was hitting him. I could have stopped. He deserved it.

FEDYA: Have it your way. *(pause)* Where will you go?

EMMA: Fedya, do you really think Sasha can survive? He's only twenty. A strong young tree, robbed of sun and light. How can it live?

(She starts to cry. Fedya puts her head on his shoulder. BLACKOUT.)

ACT ....
TWO

(Berkman in his cell, writing a letter.)

(CLOSE-UP—Letter: Allegheny City, Pa., October 19th, 1892. Berkman begins to read the letter aloud. As he does so, we see various shots of Emma.)

BERKMAN *(voice-over):*   Dearest Girl: It is just a month today, since my coming here. I keep wondering, can such a world of misery and torture be compressed into one short month? . . .

(Under voice-over: Emma entering a fleabag hotel. As she signs her name in the register, the clerk looks at it in horror, vigorously shakes his head to indicate no vacancy.)

BERKMAN *(voice-over):*   . . . a month's stay is required before we are permitted to write. But many, many long letters I have written to you— in my mind, dear Emma. Where shall I begin now? . . . I sense bitterness and disappointment in your letter. Why do you speak of failure? You, at least, you and Fedya, should not have your judgment obscured by the mere accident of physical results. Your lines pained and grieved me beyond words. Need I enlarge? True morality deals with motives, not consequences. I cannot believe that we differ on this point. . . .

(Under voice-over: Emma approaching a tenement with a Furnished Room to Rent *sign. CLOSE-UP— Owner and his wife. The woman starts to shout at Emma. The husband, in turn, yells at his wife and tries to reassure Emma. Horrified at the reception, Emma flees.)*

BERKMAN *(voice-over):*   I embrace you. The future

is dark; but then, who knows? Write often. I clutch desperately at the thread that still binds me to the living—it seems to unravel in my hands. My hold is slackening. But the Emma thread, I know, will remain taut and strong. I have always called you the Immutable.

(Under voice-over: Three in the morning. Emma riding back and forth on a horse-drawn streetcar. She has on the blue-and-white striped dress and long gray coat of a nurse's uniform. She is about to doze off when a young policeman gets on the car. He looks solicitously at Emma.)

YOUNG POLICEMAN *(in thick Irish brogue):* You look all in, kid. Workin' too hard, ain't you?

(Emma is at first panicky, then recovers her composure.)

EMMA: Yes, yes, Officer. I've been on nursing duty day and night this whole week. Only a few hours in between.

YOUNG POLICEMAN: Well now, you just doze off, and I'll wake you at your stop. Where is it you're goin'?

EMMA: Going? . . . Oh—yes. Fourth Street, sir, Fourth Street and Third Avenue.

YOUNG POLICEMAN: All right, then. You put your head right down and go off to sleep.

EMMA: Thank you, officer. You're very kind . . . very kind . . . *(closes her eyes).*

(FREEZE. As Berkman reads his letter, voice-over, MONTAGE of Emma:)

BERKMAN: November 18, 1892. The monotony of my life weighs down . . . the only break in the terrible sameness is afforded by your dear, affectionate letters, and those of Fedya. . . . The bars fade, the walls disappear. . . . I am again with you, walking in the bright July moonlight. . . . What will become of me, I don't know. I hardly care. We are revolutionists, dear: Whatever sacrifices the Cause demands, though the individual perish, humanity will profit in the end. In that consciousness we must find our solace.

(Under voice-over: Emma, carrying her suitcase, trudges along the streets of the Lower East Side, still searching for a room. Now and then she stops as if to enter a building, but a hostile face appears and she walks on. She passes a stoop. The woman sitting there gives her a warm, friendly smile, and gestures for her to come inside. Emma, astonished, follows her in. The woman shows her a small but pleasant room. Emma nods that she'll take it. She signs the register)

(CLOSE-UP—The register: Emma's hand is writing "Miss E. G. Smith.")

(CUT TO: Emma in her room. Exhausted, she has stretched out on the bed, without having unpacked. A knock at her door. Wearily she gets up.)

EMMA: Yes? Who is it?

MAN: C'mon, Vi, let me in! I been knockin' for ten minutes. What the hell is up?!

EMMA: Who are you?

MAN: Damn it, Viola, this is my night! You promised to save it.

EMMA: I'm *not* Viola.

MAN: Not Viola? What kind of a crazy dump is this?

(FREEZE. CUT TO: Emma, writing Berkman. Then Emma's voice reading the letter over scene.)

EMMA *(voice-over)*:   Then he mumbled, "What kind of a crazy dump is this?"

(CUT TO: The Buford. [scene one, act one] Emma's voice continues over MONTAGE of the Buford.)

EMMA *(voice -over)*:   I soon found out, Sasha dear: It's a brothel. But not, as one of the girls has told me, "just a regular dump, with a Madam." It's a rooming house where the girls are allowed to bring their men. Well, I'm not proud if they aren't. The girl in the next room at first refused to believe that I make my living as a dressmaker. Now that I've convinced her, she's spread the word. I've become a confidante for them. They compete with one another in being kind to me, in giving me their sewing to do and helping in little ways. I am able to earn a living. Most of them are such sad creatures.

(The Buford: The terrible conditions: cold and wet; the men locked below deck; reading material confiscated; exercise prevented; prisoners lying feverish in bunks, unattended.

Notes being passed between the men and the women with the help of a steward.

The steward walking into Emma's cabin with his hands under his apron. He produces chicken and pastry for her and the other women in the cabin. They hug and kiss him. He puts his fingers to his lips to warn them to be quiet. Emma makes sure that some of the food is set aside to be smuggled to the men.)

(CUT TO: A guard outside the cabin, pacing up and down. DISSOLVE from the guard on the Buford to a guard outside the visitors' room in Berkman's prison.)

VOICE: This way, Mrs. Niedermann.

(CAMERA picks up Emma, heavily veiled, walking toward the guard. He stops her in front of the door to the room. She hands him her papers.)

EMMA *(heavy Russian accent)*: I am Mrs. Niedermann, sister of Alexander Berkman. My visit has been cleared.

(The guard looks at the papers, then suspiciously at Emma, and finally opens the door into the visitors' room. We can see Berkman standing at the end of the room, staring straight ahead. When he catches sight of Emma, he slowly comes toward her. He reaches her and puts his arm around her. CLOSE-UP—Berkman's lips on her hand; her hand is trembling. Neither speaks. CLOSE-UP—Emma's face, drawn, sad. They exchange a few words haltingly in Russian.)

GUARD: Talk English! No foreign languages here.

(They fall silent, simply holding each other. JUMP CUT to Berkman and Emma sitting, still holding each other, still not speaking.)

GUARD: Time's up!

(Berkman lifts Emma's face to his.)

EMMA *(barely audible)*:   Hold on, Sashenka.

(He kisses her.)

(CUT TO: Guard, taking her away. CLOSE-UP— Berkman, forlorn.)

(CUT TO: Emma—in inspector's office.)

INSPECTOR: This is your first—and last—visit, *Miss Goldman.* Yes, we know who you are. The guard recognized you. You won't get away with that trick twice. The only time you'll see Berkman again is when you get jailed yourself. And in my opinion, that can't happen too soon.

(Emma, in a fury, sweeps everything off his desk: papers, inkstand, ashtrays, books fly over the room. The guards restrain her.)

INSPECTOR: Regular spitfire, eh?

EMMA *(screaming)*:   If you touch Sasha, I'll kill you! I'll kill you with my own hands!

INSPECTOR: Get her out of here. Get that vixen bitch outta here!

(FREEZE.)

(CUT TO: Guard on the Buford [scene one, act one]. *Exhausted from walking back and forth, he wearily sits down on the railing and closes his eyes. Emma comes out of the cabin and sees him. He immediately jumps up and starts pacing again, scowling fiercely at her.)*

EMMA: You must be very tired.

GUARD: I know my duty.

EMMA: Yes, you seem very conscientious. But why don't you sit for a while? I promise not to jump overboard. ˜

GUARD: I know all about you.

EMMA: Do you?

(She gets a camp chair from the cabin and puts it in front of him.)

EMMA: Then you know that I made my living as a nurse for many years, and I know nervous exhaustion when I see it. Sit. I'll keep watch for you.

GUARD: The sergeant might come along.

EMMA: I'll stand at the rail and be lookout. And if I see Alexander Berkman blowing anything up, you'll be the first to know.

(The guard sits.)

EMMA: We're heading into German waters, aren't we.

GUARD: How did you know that?

EMMA: How can you not know? The captain's had the lifeboats ready for days. First they give us an unseaworthy boat, then they head us into mine fields. I can understand their willingness to see a few hundred anarchists blown up, but you'd think the American government would have a little more regard for its own soldiers.

GUARD *(grudgingly)*: A lot of the men are grumbling.

EMMA: Yes, I know.

GUARD: You do?

EMMA: Some of your soldiers have offered to supply us with guns, to arrest the commanding officers on board and to sail with all hands directly for Russia.

GUARD: That's treason!

EMMA *(smiling)*: That's not why we refused. We don't want to risk any lives other than our own. Besides, we'll be in Russia soon enough.

GUARD: I don't believe you.

EMMA: That is your privilege.

GUARD: They gave us a full briefing on you. You're a desperado, an ex-con.

EMMA: Gossip is a good way to spend time on shipboard. The days are so long. *(they smile.)* I *was* arrested many times. For expressing my opinions. Once for advocating birth control. Once for encouraging strikers to hold out for a decent wage. Once for publishing an article against conscription in *Mother Earth*.

GUARD: Is that your nickname?

EMMA: It was the title of a magazine I ran for many years. Until President Wilson suppressed it as treasonable.

GUARD: Everywhere you go, there seems to be treason.

EMMA: That's a nice compliment, young man. Thank you.

GUARD: I guess prison can't be worse than this.

EMMA: Prison is terrible. This is, too. *(she smiles at him)* But there are human possibilities everywhere.

(FREEZE.)

(CUT TO: Police hustling Emma off a lecture platform. A man jumps up from the audience and tries to assist her. He is about forty, well-built, blond, intelligent looking.)

POLICEMAN: You're under arrest, Miss Goldman.

MAN: What's she done, for God's sakes? You can't break up a meeting for no reason!

POLICEMAN: Stay out of this, mister, or you'll go along with her.

MAN: What you're doing is against the law.

POLICEMAN: It ain't against common sense. Red Emma shoulda been in jail long ago.

(As they hustle Emma off, she calls back to the man.)

EMMA: Thank you, comrade. What is your name?

MAN: Ed Brady. I'll come see you. It was a great speech!

(CUT TO: Office of chief of police. Emma is being questioned.)

CHIEF: We've been expecting you for a long time, Miss Goldman. Frankly, I thought you'd arrive on a stretcher.

EMMA: Sorry to disappoint you.

CHIEF: If you don't behave there's a good chance you'll leave on one.

EMMA: What are the charges against me?

CHIEF: Incitement to riot.

EMMA: And the proof?

CHIEF: You seem a smart woman, Miss Goldman. It's possible that if you promise to leave New York—and never return—we might drop the charges.

EMMA: I doubt if your city can do without me for

very long. Besides, I want no charges dropped. I want them *specified*.

CHIEF: There is another possibility. We might be interested in periodic reports on what's going on in radical circles. Nothing elaborate. They'd be held in strictest confidence. No one need ever know that you—

(Emma grabs the glass of water on the chief's desk and throws the water at him full in the face.)

EMMA: I'd go to prison for life before I'd act Judas for you and your kind!

CHIEF: Perhaps we can arrange exactly that!

(Guards grab Emma. She struggles. FREEZE. DIS-SOLVE OUT: Emma is still struggling, now it is against being photographed. The guards finally pinion her head. Just before the bulb goes off, she closes her eyes in defiance.)

(CUT TO: Emma in prison clothes, being interro-gated by the matron.)

MATRON: If you behave decently, the parole board might cut the year sentence to eleven months. It's up to you.

EMMA: How generous! Only eleven months for the crime of speaking my mind.

MATRON *(abruptly)*: Any disease?

EMMA: I could use a bath, if that's what you mean.

MATRON: Don't be impudent. And don't pretend

you don't know what I mean. Most of the women who arrive here have venereal disease.

EMMA: So do many "respectable" people. I don't happen to have it, which is due more to luck than virtue.

MATRON: What religion?

EMMA: I'm an atheist.

MATRON: Atheism is prohibited. You must attend some religious service regularly.

EMMA: I'll do nothing of the kind! The church is an instrument of enslavement.

(The matron walks away.)

EMMA: Just a minute. I have certain rights, and I know them. I want my mail. And I want reading material.

(The matron picks up a Bible lying on the table and hands it to Emma.)

MATRON: This, I think, will keep you profitably occupied.

(Emma looks at the book, then throws it at the feet of the matron.)

EMMA: I want a *human* book.

MATRON *(exploding):* You desecrate God's word! You'll burn in hell!

EMMA: I burn wherever I go, madam. It's a matter of principle.

(FREEZE.)

(CUT TO: Emma, at her sewing machine in the prison shop. She and Aggie, a black woman operating the machine next to her, are whispering.)

AGGIE: The girls said to thank you for the fruit.

EMMA: I had much more than I could eat. Fedya sent a whole case.

AGGIE: Who did?

EMMA: An old friend. *(watching with amazement the speed with which Aggie works)* Aggie, how do you do it so fast? I'm exhausted.

AGGIE: Got to stay Grade A. Means two months off the sentence every year. Won't help you federals none; no reduction time for federals. But you better make the task, or you get no letter writin', and maybe the blind cell.

(Emma rubs her neck and closes her eyes in pain.)

AGGIE: Don't fret, honey. I always make the task by three. I'll help you make yours.

EMMA: Oh, thanks, Aggie. My mail means so much to me. Maybe you'd let me give you a little money for helping.

AGGIE *(indignant):*   What you talkin' 'bout? I don't take no money from people ah like!

EMMA: I'm sorry.

AGGIE: Fruit, candies, cakes. You practically feedin' this place.

EMMA: Friends keep sending them. I'm glad to share with my sisters.

AGGIE: You got good friends, Emma. Any of 'em black?

EMMA: Not till you, Aggie.

AGGIE *(giving her a big grin)*: Ooh—you somethin'! You gotta be in here for dope! *(they laugh).* S-sh!—here she come.

(The matron strides up.)

MATRON: As if you didn't know, Miss Goldman, no talking is allowed.

(Emma holds up the label she's been sewing.)

EMMA: I was only saying to Aggie how fitting it is that convict, slave labor is used to sew on these particular labels.

(CLOSE-UP—Label. It is a picture of Abe Lincoln. Above his face, the words, "Lincoln Jobbing House of Milwaukee." Below his face the legend, "True to his country, true to our trade.")

(CUT TO: Emma, alone in her cell. She's reading a letter from Berkman. We hear his voice as she reads it.)

BERKMAN *(voice-over)*: So now you've joined us,

old jailmate! We're putting out a sub rosa prison paper here. Its name is *Prison Blossoms*. Each page is three inches by five. I write a page and pass it to K. He reads mine, adds a page of his own, then passes both to M, who likewise—

(Emma is interrupted by a guard's voice at her cell door.)

GUARD: Visitor! Ten minutes.

(Ed Brady walks in.)

BRADY: Miss Goldman . . .

EMMA: Mr. Brady!

BRADY: You remember me . . . I'm so glad.

EMMA: A pity we have to meet again here.

BRADY *(looking around)*: It feels quite like home. I spent ten years in prison.

EMMA: For *what*?

BRADY: Publishing illegal anarchist literature. In Austria.

EMMA: Ten years! How did you stand it?

BRADY: I was already thirty. Not as young as you—or your friend Berkman. It's easier when you're older. You care more about books. I studied a lot.

EMMA: Well, I'm awfully ignorant, but I can't get

any books in here. The matron seems to feel the Bible is the sum of all knowledge. Still, they keep us busy, Mr. Brady.

BRADY: "Mr. Brady" sounds so conventional— especially from you. Won't you call me Ed?

EMMA: All right. (*laughs*) How nice to be considered conventional!

BRADY: I'm sure they keep you busy. Convict labor's a profitable business.

EMMA: They tried to put me in charge of the sewing shop. I told the matron I'd been sent to prison because I hated slave drivers, and had no intention of becoming one myself in here.

BRADY: I'm surprised she didn't put you in the dungeon for that.

EMMA: She threatened to. Fortunately I took sick. And the most wonderful thing happened. The doctor in the prison hospital arranged for me to become his nurse.

BRADY: You have a lot of experience taking care of people.

EMMA (*ignoring the implication*): Dr. Rogers is a wonderful man. When he came to my bed that first day, he picked up the card giving my crime and said, "'Inciting a riot'—piffle! I don't believe you could hurt a fly." He and the priest have become my best friends.

BRADY: The *priest*?

EMMA: We have long talks—about everything but religion. Our faiths are at opposite poles; fervor is the meeting ground. But tell me more about yourself.

BRADY: Well, let's see. I'm trying to learn French. I like to cook. I'm said to be reserved. I never speak of love. I think sex is a life-giving force. I work in the wood shop of a Hungarian friend. And . . .

EMMA: And?

BRADY: And I'm going to marry you when you get out of prison.

(Emma bursts out laughing.)

EMMA: I thought you were going to say: "And I, too, am an anarchist."

BRADY: I am.

EMMA: And you want to *marry*?

BRADY: Everyone has his weakness.

(Emma laughs again. The guard appears at the door.)

GUARD: Time's up!

EMMA: I like you, Ed. You're not reserved.

(CLOSE-UP of Brady bending down and kissing Emma's hand.)

(FREEZE on her hand. UNFREEZE: Her hand is on

*a patient's arm in the prison hospital. As Emma
makes her rounds we hear Berkman [voice-over].)*

BERKMAN *(voice-over)*:   April 12, 1896. I can't pro-
cure a permit for friends to visit me. . . . The
warden has conceived a great fear of an anarchist plot against the prison . . . purportedly
because a "certain anarchist lady" threatened
him. . . . Fedya writes seldom nowadays. But
you are never disappointing. It is not so much
the contents that matter; these increasingly
sound, after four years in here, like the language
of a strange world, with its bewildering flurry
and ferment. But I'm glad to hear you have
productive work in the hospital prison, helping
those in need.

*(We hear a piercing scream. DISSOLVE TO: Emma
rushing toward the sounds. CLOSE-UP—A tearful
prisoner pleading with Emma.)*

WOMAN: Please, Emma, *please.* Just a whiff,
that's all. Who would find out?

*(Emma takes the woman's face in her hands. She
herself is near tears.)*

EMMA: Oh, Kate dear, you know I would if I could.

WOMAN: I can't stand the pain, Emma. Just a drop
of morphine. A drop would do it. (*puts her head
in Emma's lap and starts to moan*) For the love
of Christ, Emma!

EMMA *(stroking her head)*:   My poor darling. It
isn't human to cut you off like they've done. But
Dr. Rogers put his faith in me. What can I do?

WOMAN *(almost incoherent)*:   My children, what's to become of my poor children?

EMMA: Come, darling. Let me put you back in bed. I'll stay with you, I promise.

(As Emma half carries the woman to her bed, FREEZE.)

(DISSOLVE OUT INTO: Emma, sitting by a woman's bed in a squalid tenement room. The woman starts to thrash about and moan.)

IRISH WOMAN *(brogue)*:   A curse of God . . . A curse of God . . .

EMMA *(soothing her)*:   There, Mrs. Mulcahy . . . you're out of danger now. . . . It's all over.

IRISH WOMAN: Did the brat live? . . . Did it live?

EMMA: The little thing's only four pounds. But she'll live.

IRISH WOMAN *(groaning again)*:   It's your fault. You shouldn'ta stopped me. . . .

EMMA: You almost killed yourself.

IRISH WOMAN: And who's to care . . . six brats I can't feed already. Ah, the rich ones don't need to swallow the brew or jump off a table. Them's the only ways we got—that and fighting off the old man every night. . . .

EMMA: You can't leave your children motherless.

IRISH WOMAN: They'd be better off. The city's sure

to take care of an orphan. You can't think I'm all daft; you must have a brood of your own.

EMMA: I haven't any children.

IRISH WOMAN: Ah saints, ain't some of us lucky. . . .

(CLOSE-UP—*Emma's unhappy expression.*)

(CUT TO: *Emma and Brady, walking excitedly through a vacant apartment.*)

EMMA: Aren't we lucky, Ed?! Four whole rooms!

BRADY: I'm as happy as you are, love. But it's going to take a lot of sewing.

(CLOSE-UP—*Emma, peeking into one of the vacant rooms.*)

EMMA: I'll make this one mine. It's the smallest. I can do most of the sewing right here.

BRADY: You mean your work room.

EMMA: I have to have a room to myself, Ed. Work and sleeping. Try to understand.

BRADY: I don't understand. You say you love me.

EMMA: Oh I do, Ed. Truly. It was *my* idea we find a place.

BRADY: But then why? . . .

EMMA: I've never had privacy. Even as a little girl. And in prison, not a moment to myself . . . ever.

BRADY (*takes her in his arms*):   I want to make a home for you. For us.

EMMA: So do I, Ed. You know that.

BRADY: But you're never *in* it. Nursing cases, lectures for the Cause, protest meetings to get Sasha paroled . . .

EMMA: But you share all my ideals.

BRADY: I learned a lot in prison, Emma. I still believe in the beauty of our anarchist vision. It will triumph some day. But the time is far, far off. We can't look for great changes in our lifetime. All we can do is arrange our own lives as nearly true to the vision as possible.

EMMA: That's what we *are* doing! What are you saying, Ed? That you'd be happier if I stayed home all the time?

BRADY: I'm worried about your safety. You're so intense, so impetuous.

(*CLOSE-UP—Emma, annoyed.*)

BRADY: Don't be angry with me, but dearest, you're meant to be a mother. You're a typical mother, my little Emma, by build, by feelings. Your tenderness is the greatest proof of that.

EMMA: I've told you, Ed: The doctor said I can never have a child. That is, without an operation. And I won't have the operation. (*suddenly angry*) Men can consecrate themselves to an ideal *and* be fathers. Women must *choose!* Well, I've chosen. I *want* a child; desperately sometimes. But I won't give up all of humanity to become absorbed in a single human being. (*embraces him*) Please try to understand.

(FREEZE.)

(CUT TO: Apartment interior. A woman slamming down an open window. She screams at Emma.)

WOMAN: You're trying to kill my child! An open window at night is poison! What kind of a nurse are you?!

EMMA: Your *child*, madam, is eighteen years old. And fresh air is the best treatment for a tubercular.

WOMAN: I don't want to hear theories. Just do your job.

(She stalks from the room. Emma sinks wearily into a chair next to the patient's bed. She closes her eyes.)

(JUMP CUT TO: Emma opening her eyes with a start. A man's weight is on top of her. He presses his lips to her breast and caresses her body. She struggles frantically to push him off. Suddenly she realizes it's her boy patient.)

EMMA: Stop it—stop it! Are you mad? I'll scream for your mother!

(The boy, his eyes feverish, retreats.)

BOY: No, please . . . I don't know what happened . . . please, I . . .

(He's shaken by a paroxysm of coughing, almost falls to the floor. Emma rushes to help him, guiding him back to the bed. He clutches her hand desperately, refusing to release it.)

BOY: I'm sorry . . . oh, I'm so sorry . . .

EMMA: It's all right, it's all right . . . I understand . . . really, I understand . . .

(The boy starts to cry.)

BOY: You seem so alive. I . . . I had to touch you . . . I didn't mean any harm . . . I . . . didn't . . .

(He starts to cough again. The cough gives way to a hemorrhage. As Emma goes to assist him, FREEZE on the boy's face. DISSOLVE IN on the face of another eighteen year old, shouting. CAMERA PULLS BACK INTO: an audience of college students. They are yelling up at Emma, who stands on a lecture platform.)

VOICES: Bomb thrower . . . Free lover! This is a university, not a brothel! . . . Throw her out!

(CLOSE-UP—Emma, folding her arms. She stands quietly, showing no nervousness or impatience as the noise continues. Finally, during a lull, she steps forward.)

EMMA: I can see you young gentlemen are in a sporting mood. You want a contest. Very well, you shall have it. Go on with the noise; that will be your effort. And when you've stopped, I'll give you mine.

(The audience, surprised, quiets down.)

VOICE: All right—let's hear it!

EMMA: I don't think your behavior today should be ascribed to the high spirits of youth. Nor to any intentional wish to hurt. I see it simply as the effects on you of authority. Everywhere in our society the cry is, "thou shalt not!", everywhere we hear the command to obey. From cradle to grave, we're controlled and dictated to.

(Some scattered applause.)

EMMA: Society turns on an endless cycle of domination and submission, of command and obedience, of coercion and subjection, of rulers and ruled. Nowhere more so than here in the university. You're taught to be parrots, to repeat time-worn slogans. You can no longer think for yourselves or feel social wrongs.

(More applause.)

EMMA: I came to you as a stranger, expecting kindness and hospitality. I came expecting the free exchange of opinions. But how could I have when authority—in the school, the home, the body politic—has so long bent its energy to destroying those possibilities in you? I believe in the possibilities of youth. And you are young, gentlemen, very, very young. That's fortunate, because you're still impressionable. Put the energy you've shown this afternoon to better use. Put it toward a better future.

(The audience breaks into a college yell.)

(CUT TO: Emma and Brady, in James Huneker's living room.)

HUNEKER: . . . I agree with your enthusiasm for Ibsen. The hater of all social sham.

EMMA: I mean especially the sham of "wifely duty." Nora's lines to her husband tell it all: "When I look back on it now, I seem to have been living like a beggar, from hand to mouth. I lived by performing tricks for you." When Nora closes the door of her gilded cage behind her, she opens up the gate of freedom for her sex.

BRADY: Huneker said he agreed with you. Why the speech? You're with friends, not undergraduates.

(CLOSE-UP—Emma, startled and hurt.)

HUNEKER: It's your enthusiasm for Nietzsche that surprises me.

BRADY: Huneker thinks you're interested only in propaganda.

EMMA: That's because Huneker—like you—doesn't understand that anarchism embraces every phase of life, and every honest effort to undermine outlived values.

HUNEKER: Art has nothing to do with any "ism."

Nietzsche himself is the proof. He's an aristocrat, unconcerned with the common man.

EMMA: He's not an aristocrat by birth or wealth, but by spirit. He's a rebel, an innovator. And that makes him an anarchist.

BRADY: Nietzsche's a fool. A man with a diseased mind. He'll be forgotten in a decade. A *pseudo*-modern, a contortionist.

EMMA (*outraged*):   You haven't even read Nietzsche!

BRADY: I've read all of him—all his silly books.

(CLOSE-UP—*Emma's startled face. FREEZE.*)

(*UNFREEZE on her face, angry. She and Brady are now back in their apartment.*)

EMMA: It isn't Nietzsche—it's *you*! Under the pre-text of love, you want to chain me, bind me. The books I love, my work for the movement—you want to tear them all from me.

BRADY: Applause, glory, the limelight—that's what you want! Your life with me means nothing in comparison.

EMMA: I thought I was working for things we *both* believed in.

BRADY: I won't share you with anything or any-body. You'll have to choose.

EMMA: What a familiar sound that has.

BRADY: Every man feels the same.

EMMA: Almost every man. But not Sasha.

BRADY: Your precious Sasha.

EMMA *(blazing)*:   Sasha's locked in prison—but understands our love. You're free—and choose to make for us a prison.

BRADY: I need you, Emma. I need our home.

EMMA: Then be big enough to accept what I freely offer.

BRADY: I love Emma Goldman, the woman.

EMMA: The woman and her ideas are one. You're rooted in the old. Well, stay there. But don't think you can hold me there with you. I'll free myself even if it means tearing you out of my heart.

(FREEZE.)

(CUT TO: Berkman's cell. He's stroking a bird that he's tamed. As he goes to get it some water, the bird hops into the corridor. A guard comes by.)

GUARD: That damned bird again! The warden told you to put him out. We're not running a goddam zoo here!

(He gives the bird a vicious kick. It rolls over on its side in a death throe. Berkman starts to scream.)

(FREEZE.)

(CUT TO: Emma, waking up.)

BERKMAN *(voice-over)*:   I lost control when I saw

the guard kill the sparrow, and when he entered my cell I attacked him. He wasn't hurt, but the warden ordered me put into the straitjacket. They bound my body in canvas, strapped my arms to the bed, and chained my feet to the posts.

(Under Berkman's voice-over, Emma hears crashing noises in the next room. She opens her door a crack and looks out. The living room is littered with broken furniture. Brady throws himself on the couch and passes out.)

BERKMAN *(voice-over)*: The guard came by a few times every night and tightened the straps. I thought he'd cut my hands off; but I wouldn't cry for mercy, and that made him wild. I was suffocating. My legs were paralyzed. I was kept that way eight days, unable to move, rotting in my own excrement. Reports spread that I was going blind and insane.

(CUT TO: Brady asleep in bed. Emma and Fedya are nearby, talking in low tones. Fedya is noticeably older and more prosperously dressed. He presses some money into Emma's hand. She tries to refuse it, but he insists.)

BERKMAN *(voice-over)*: Then the inspector visited the hospital and had me released from the jacket. I'm in pretty bad shape, but they put me in the general ward now, and I'm glad of the chance to send you this note.

(CUT TO: Brady, as he takes a box of morphine from his night table. He empties out one potion, hesitates, then empties out five and swallows them all.)

BERKMAN *(voice-over)*: After years of prison, I grow indifferent to life. My whole being longs for rest. The world wouldn't miss me. I'd return to endless space. But suicide isn't in my nature. I'm determined to survive and see the day of my release. Love to you and to Ed.

(CUT TO: Emma and Fedya, under the above, asleep on the chair and sofa near Brady's bed. Emma goes over to check on Brady. Seeing his heavy breathing, she takes his pulse. Suddenly alarmed, she rouses Fedya.)

(CUT TO: Emma and Fedya, supporting Brady's weight, struggling to keep him on his feet, walking him back and forth. Emma applies ice to his hands and face.)

(JUMP CUT TO: The next morning. Brady is sitting up in a chair, with a robe over him. He's alert. Emma is preparing soup.)

EMMA: The doctor wouldn't believe it. He said you're too strong to have done such a thing.

BRADY: The doctor's right.

EMMA: What?

BRADY: I knew from past experience that I could stand large doses of morphine.

EMMA: But then . . . ? I don't understand.

BRADY: I thought to scare you a little, maybe cure your mania for meetings.

(CLOSE-UP—Emma, near tears.)

EMMA: Is that what my work means to you, Ed—a "mania for meetings"?

BRADY: I want you more now than even in the early days.

(Emma goes over to him and quietly takes his hand.)

EMMA: You want me as your wife. I need someone who believes in what I do.

BRADY: Love has nothing to do with any "ism". You'll find that out as you grow older.

EMMA: Let's part while we're friends, Ed. Before bitterness poisons what we still have.

BRADY: Our love hasn't been much of a success, has it?

EMMA: Perhaps it might last if we have the sense to separate. I'm going on tour anyway; it's the easiest time to make a break.

BRADY: I think you're wrong, Emma, terribly wrong.

(FREEZE on Emma's ambivalent expression. UN-FREEZE as it solidifies into anger. She is on the lecture platform.)

EMMA: America's declaration of war against Spain is inspired not by humanitarian feelings for the Cuban people but by a desire to expand our sugar market. *(protest noises from the audience)* War itself is barbarism, but to clothe it in protestations of humanity is sickening. If Cuba becomes free, it will be despite our efforts, not because of them. No government engaged in enslaving and exploiting its own people at home is likely to be sincere in its desire to free people elsewhere.

(Bedlam in the audience.)

EMMA: Don't bellow like calves! Talk like men! Let's have one of you brave lads up here to speak his mind. What we want is to hear both sides, isn't it?

VOICE: Betcher life!

EMMA: Besides, I've never been good at keeping order. Maybe one of you men can.

(An elderly man, elegantly dressed, steps up to the platform. He bangs his cane fiercely on the table.)

ELDERLY MAN *(shouting)*:   *Silence!* I wish to hear what this woman has to say!

(The crowd becomes quiet. Emma gives the man a sweeping bow, then turns to the audience.)

EMMA: You see, gentlemen, I've been proven partly wrong already—the country is *not* entirely devoid of humanitarian sentiment!

(Loud laughter from the audience.)

(FREEZE.)

(CUT TO: Emma, backstage, examining a huge bouquet of American Beauty roses. She's puzzling

over the card attached to them. A knock on the door. She opens it. A middle-aged, attractive, well-groomed man [Peter Yamin] is standing there.)

EMMA: Yes?

YAMIN: Peter Yamin, Miss Goldman. May I come in?

EMMA: Peter—? *(looks again at the card)* Oh yes, Mr. Yamin. Thank you for the flowers. They're lovely.

YAMIN: You probably don't remember me. But we met once at Justus Schwab's in New York.

EMMA: Frankly, I can't say that—

YAMIN: —It's no matter. I've come to offer my services. I've been to every one of your lectures in Cincinnati. I want to help.

EMMA: That's very kind. But help in what way?

YAMIN: I'm often in California on business, and have many contacts there. I've heard you can't find a hall to speak in Los Angeles.

EMMA *(laughing):*   Yes. The anarchist comrades there have advised me not to come. They don't approve of some of my lectures, especially on the sex question. They think I make their work more difficult.

YAMIN: I'd be honored if you would allow me to act as your manager in Los Angeles.

EMMA: Are you an anarchist?

YAMIN: I'm becoming one. I need your help. And I can offer help in return.

EMMA: I'd be a fool to scorn a friend *and* a potential convert. Especially one armed with roses.

(They smile at each other.)

(FREEZE.)

(CUT TO: A luxurious hotel room in Los Angeles. Roses are everywhere. Emma paces the room in bewilderment.)

EMMA: I don't understand. Are managers always so solicitous?

YAMIN: If they know their business—and like their artists.

EMMA: This is all much too glamorous. It doesn't suit me, or my purpose.

YAMIN: I've rented the best theater in town. Advertisements are everywhere.

EMMA: Peter—no, no, this must stop. I'm not a fashion plate. This is all wrong.

YAMIN: Don't you want the meeting to be a success?

EMMA: What does that have to do with staying in fancy hotels?

YAMIN: A great deal. It will advertise the lecture.

EMMA: In the wrong way.

YAMIN: This is why you reach so few people! Now—look at this! (*holds up a beautiful black chiffon dress*) For you. To wear at the lecture.

(*Emma fingers the dress admiringly.*)

EMMA: It's like in the fairy tales Mama would read me as a child. (*recovers herself*) Is this to be a lecture or a wedding?

YAMIN: A lecture first.

EMMA (*putting the dress down*): No, it's vanity, simply vanity. It's against everything I stand for.

YAMIN: Emma, *you want to reach people.* Ask your male friends. They'll tell you a nice dress and fine hairdo is more important than the best speech.

(*CLOSE-UP—Emma, hesitant.*)

YAMIN: Now be sensible. You agreed to let me manage the affair. A bargain's a bargain.

(*CUT TO: Emma on the platform, wearing the black chiffon dress. The hall is packed and enthusiastic.*)

EMMA: . . . What does anyone know of human nature?! To deduce human nature from human history is like discussing lions only after studying those caged up in a zoo. That is all human history shows—what human nature is like caged in a narrow space, whipped daily into submission. How can we know what it is capable of until all the cages are thrown open, until we are free to explore, free from the constrictions of religion and property and government? . . .

(Resounding applause.)

(CLOSE-UP—The face of an intense young man [Czolgosz] in the audience, his eyes gleaming. FREEZE.)

(CUT TO: A hotel room. Emma is back in her ordinary clothes. She folds the chiffon dress and hands it to Yamin.)

YAMIN: But it was marvelous! You heard the response!

EMMA: I was another toy. It's degrading to me, and to them. A silly charade.

YAMIN: But you looked so *pretty*!

EMMA: That's the silliest part of all.

(As she hands him back the dress, FREEZE.)

(UNFREEZE on Emma back in plain clothes on the lecture platform.)

EMMA: . . . Patriotism is a superstition—and one far more brutal and inhumane than religion. Religion at least originates in man's inability to explain natural phenomena. Patriotism, on the other hand, is created artificially and maintained through lies.

(CUT TO: The tall figure of a soldier in uniform in the audience; he's visibly agitated.)

EMMA: Those born on one particular spot are taught to consider themselves better, nobler, grander, more intelligent than the living beings inhabiting any other spot. It is, therefore, the duty of those living on that chosen spot to fight, kill, and die in the attempt to impose their "superiority" upon all the others. Leo Tolstoy is right: Patriotism is the principle that justifies the training of wholesale murderers.

(Thunderous applause. The crowd presses around Emma to congratulate her, the soldier also. Almost involuntarily, he holds out his hand to her. She takes it. With that, pandemonium breaks loose; people throw their hats in the air, stamp their feet, shout their approval.)

SOLDIER: Thank you, Miss Goldman.

(CUT TO: The Buford (scene one, act one). Emma is in conversation with the young guard still seated on the camp chair.)

EMMA: Yes, you'd think the American government would have a little more regard for its own soldiers.

GUARD: I guess he shouldn't have shook your hand in public like that. I mean, him in uniform and all.

EMMA: That's just what the court-martial sentence said: "For the crime of attending Emma Goldman's meeting in uniform, applauding her speech, and shaking hands with that dangerous anarchist woman, you are hereby sentenced to five years in the military prison on Alcatraz Island."

GUARD: Five years?!

EMMA: He later told me he'd wandered into the meeting by accident, while out for a walk. And had disagreed with most of what I said. Still, I'd made him think, and so he wanted to shake my hand. In prison he thought a lot more. He returned the medal he'd been awarded for "faithful service" in the Philippines. He sent me a copy of his letter to the War Department. I've quoted it many times since when lecturing. I know it by heart: "To the Honorable Joseph M. Dickinson, Secretary of War, Washington, D.C."

(As Emma continues to quote the letter, CAMERA DISSOLVES from the Buford and her voice continues over a MONTAGE.)

EMMA *(voice-over):*   "I have decided to send back this trinket to your department. . . . It speaks to me of faithful service, of duty well done, of friendships inseparable, friendships cemented by dangers and hardships and sufferings shared in common in camp and in the field. But, sir, it also speaks to me of bloodshed . . . it speaks of raids and burnings, of many prisoners taken and, like vile beasts, thrown in the foulest of prisons . . ."

(MONTAGE:

Emma on the lecture platform.

Emma, after a speech, being handed a wreath of huge red carnations by a tiny golden-haired child who is all but blotted out by the bouquet. Emma picks up the child, presses her to her heart, and carries her off—bouquet and all.

Emma laying the bouquet on the monument to the

Haymarket martyrs at Waldheim Cemetery [Chicago]. Fedya is with her.)

EMMA *(voice-over):* ". . . it speaks to me of a country laid waste with fire and sword, of animals useful to man wantonly killed; of men, women, and children hunted like wild beasts, and all this in the name of Liberty, Humanity, and Civilization. . . . In short, it speaks to me of War—legalized murder, if you will—upon a weak and defenseless people. We have not even the excuse of self-defense. Yours sincerely, William Buwalda, R. R. Number 3, Hudsonville, Michigan."

(CUT TO: Emma, walking on the street. She's brought up short by the shouts of a newsboy.)

NEWSBOY: Extra! Extra! President McKinley shot! Extra! Extra! Read all about it! President McKinley shot twice at Exposition grounds in Buffalo!

(DISSOLVE TO: Emma's apartment. Several friends are there, including Fedya, Brady, and Anya.)

FEDYA: You *must* leave the city, Emma. They're bound to try to implicate you.

EMMA: But *why*, for heaven's sake? I wasn't in Buffalo. I've never heard of the poor boy— Choogosh, Choogosh—I can't even pronounce his name.

ANYA: Czolgosz. Leon Czolgosz.

FEDYA: Emma, for years they've wanted an excuse

to lock you up again. Czolgosz has declared himself an anarchist. That's all they need.

EMMA: The American press may be dishonest, but it wouldn't invent a story from scratch.

BRADY: Emma: look.

(CLOSE-UP—Newspaper in Brady's hand:

September 6, 1901

ASSASSIN OF PRESIDENT MCKINLEY AN ANARCHIST. CONFESSES TO HAVING BEEN INCITED BY EMMA GOLDMAN. WOMAN ANARCHIST WANTED.)

ANYA: They've rounded up dozens of comrades already. The authorities have said all will be held until Emma Goldman is found.

EMMA: Then I'll turn myself in at once. There isn't a shred of evidence. I'll be freed in an hour.

BRADY: Czolgosz has admitted hearing you speak earlier this year in Los Angeles. The papers have already converted that into your having inspired him. It could be enough to hang you.

FEDYA: Emma, I beg you; it's Haymarket all over again. If you turn yourself in, you'll never come out alive.

BRADY: Your one hope is Canada. The Norrises can hide you tonight. No one would think to look for you in their fashionable neighborhood. Tomorrow we can make arrangements for Canada.

(Pause.)

EMMA: All right. I'll go the Norrises. Beyond that, I don't know. The rest isn't clear yet. What will happen to Czolgosz if I escape? Things will go hard for him.

FEDYA: If McKinley lives, Czolgosz will be all right.

EMMA: "All right"? Ah, Fedya, think of those words in terms of Sasha. Nine long years in prison.

ANYA: They say Czolgosz is mad.

EMMA: That's always the comfortable explanation. Come, help me destroy my letters and papers. No one else must be implicated.

(As they begin to gather and burn Emma's papers, DISSOLVE TO: Police headquarters. Czolgosz is being grilled. He shows signs of having been badly beaten. He's frightened and cowed. He speaks in broken English.)

OFFICER: You took an oath to kill the president, didn't you? Hey—you! Look up! You swore to kill the president, didn't you.

CZOLGOSZ: No, sir.

OFFICER: Louder!

CZOLGOSZ: I done my duty. I knew I would be catched.

OFFICER: Did you hear Emma Goldman speak in Los Angeles?

CZOLGOSZ: Yes, sir.

OFFICER: You heard her say it would be a good thing if all rulers were wiped off the face of the earth, didn't you?

CZOLGOSZ: She no say that.

(A second officer grabs him by the collar.)

OFFICER: Listen, Czolgosz, her speech is on record. You know what happens when you lie?

CZOLGOSZ: She no say president. She say she no believe in government. Say all government bad.

OFFICER: And anyone who represented the government oughta be destroyed, right?

CZOLGOSZ: She no say that.

OFFICER: When did she put the idea in your head to kill the president? Was it in Los Angeles?

CZOLGOSZ: My idea. *My* idea. No one tell me.

OFFICER: Why are you shielding her, Czolgosz?! It's you who'll go to the electric chair. She's already denounced you as a loafer and a nut.

(CLOSE-UP—Czolgosz, startled and hurt. He then composes himself.)

CZOLGOSZ: It no matter. She have nothing to do with my act. My idea. My act. I did for American people.

(CUT TO: The Norris home, the next morning. The Norrises are saying good-bye to Emma at the door.)

NORRIS: We'll only be gone a few hours. Fedya will be here soon with clothes to disguise you.

MRS. NORRIS: If anyone else calls, remember that you're the maid, that we're gone for the day.

EMMA: Yes, yes. Now stop worrying so much.

(They embrace. Emma closes the door behind them. She goes into the bathroom and starts running the bath water. She stops for a second as if she hears a sound coming from the next room, but then dismisses it and starts to take off her robe. Suddenly there's a loud crash of glass from the other room. Emma hurriedly throws her robe on and goes inside.)

(CLOSE-UP—A man clutching at the windowsill with one hand and holding a gun with the other.)

EMMA: Look out, you'll break your neck!

MAN: Are you deaf, lady? Why in the hell didn't you open your door?

EMMA: No hear.

(The man climbs in, then goes and opens the front door. Another dozen men crowd in. Their captain grabs Emma.)

CAPTAIN: Who are you?

EMMA: I not speak English. Swedish servant-girl.

CAPTAIN *(releasing her; to his men):*   Search everywhere. The closets, the basement, the garden, everywhere. We know she was here. (*to Emma*) Where are the Norrises?

EMMA: Miss go shop. Mister go newspaper; type-type.

(The captain takes out a picture of Emma Goldman and shoves it in front of her.)

CAPTAIN: See this?

EMMA: Yes. Pretty woman.

CAPTAIN: Has she been here?

(CLOSE SHOT—Some of the men emptying small cartons they've found in the closets.)

EMMA: No, never see. (*gesturing to men going through cartons*) Look like big woman. No find in small box.

CAPTAIN: Oh shut up!

(He pushes her out of the way. One of the policemen calls out.)

POLICEMAN: Hey, Captain Schuettler, come here and look at this! (*holds up a fountain pen*)

(CLOSE-UP—Fountain pen, with initials E.G. clearly engraved on it.)

CAPTAIN: Then she *was* here! And she'll be back. Miller, Richardson, hide yourselves in the upstairs rooms. Hagerty, into the basement. Malone, station yourself behind the—

EMMA *(interrupting)*:   —Captain Schuettler.

CAPTAIN: I told you to stay out of the way.

EMMA: I am Emma Goldman.

CAPTAIN *(startled)*:   Well, I'll be damned! That was quite a performance.

EMMA: Mmm. They say I have a flair for the stage. But there's no point carrying this charade to the point where you destroy the Norrises' home and reputation.

CAPTAIN: Grab her! Quick!

(As the policemen seize Emma, DISSOLVE TO: Emma, undergoing interrogation at the jail.)

CAPTAIN: Don't tell us you weren't with Czolgosz! I seen you there with my own eyes. Do ya hear me?—with my own eyes!

EMMA: They must be remarkable for distance, Captain Schuettler, since at the time I was in St. Louis.

ANOTHER OFFICER: Keep this up, and you'll get the chair, Goldman. Your lover, Czolgosz, has already confessed; he admits it was under your influence that he shot the president.

EMMA: My *lover*! I've seen the newspaper pictures, gentlemen, of that poor, frail boy. He's not—as you might say—my "type." Besides, I refuse to believe he's made any confession involving me in any way. No one with so frank a face would be so craven.

CAPTAIN: The whole country knows you're a murderess.

EMMA: It's a tragedy, Captain Schuettler, to have a fool in the family, but to have fifty million maniacs in a nation is a calamity.

(FREEZE.)

(CUT TO: Emma, in her cell, a barred enclosure exposed to view on every side.)

MATRON *(kindly)*: No supper at all?

EMMA: First some water, please. I haven't had a drop all day.

MATRON: *What?*—they had you in there ten hours!

EMMA: Yes, and through it all kept a large pitcher of water on the table right in front of me. All I had to do was "confess," and I could drink my fill. (*matron helps her drink from tin cup*) This is a cage, not a cell. It's exposed on every side.

MATRON: I'll dim the lights. Maybe you can get some rest. Then I'll get you some supper.

EMMA: Thank you. You're kind.

(Lights dim. Emma stretches out on a cot and dozes off.)

(JUMP CUT TO: Emma's eyes, suddenly opening. A glaring reflector is being held directly in front of her face. Emma pushes the officer away.)

EMMA: You're burning my eyes, you fool!

OFFICER: We'll burn more than that before we get through with you.

(Captain Schuettler enters the cell.)

CAPTAIN *(smiling smugly)*:   We've got all we need now, Goldman. Not only were you and Czolgosz lovers, but you yourself financed the whole assassination.

EMMA *(wistfully amused)*:   Your facts are a little out of date. And the names.

CAPTAIN: What's that supposed to mean?

EMMA: Never mind. Well, since you have all the evidence you need, perhaps you'll let me get some rest.

CAPTAIN: That's all you got to say?

EMMA: I've said everything already. I know nothing about Czolgosz's act.

(The matron enters the cell, carrying a tray of food and some letters. Emma eagerly goes for the letters).

(CLOSE-UP—The letters; Emma sees that they've all been slit and examined.)

EMMA: You have no right to open my mail! That's a matter of law—and you're supposedly its defenders!

(She sweeps the letters onto the floor.)

(CLOSE-UP—Schuettler, as he picks up a few.)

CAPTAIN *(snide)*:   Now, now, don't be hasty. Some of these contain very beautiful sentiments. *(reading from one)* "I wish I could get at you, you damned bitch of an anarchist. I'd tear your heart out and feed it to my dog." This one is even sweeter: "We will cut your tongue out, soak your carcass in oil, and burn you alive."

EMMA: I suggest you send them to a psychiatrist. I'm told they specialize in perversion.

(The officers turn angrily to leave. The captain slams the cell gate behind him.)

CAPTAIN: We'll get you, you bitch.

(Emma sits down exhausted on her cot. The matron comes over with the tray of food, and whisks off the napkin covering it.)

MATRON: Now have a look at this!

(CLOSE-UP—The tray. It's a sumptuous turkey dinner with all the trimmings, including wine and flowers.)

EMMA *(startled)*:   What—?!

MATRON: From Mac, the saloon-keeper around the corner.

EMMA: Who is he—and why should he do this?

MATRON: We're all Democrats, and McKinley's a Republican. Mac's the ward heeler and hates the Republicans worse than the devil.

EMMA: You don't mean you're glad McKinley was shot?

MATRON: Not glad exactly. Not sorry, neither. We have to pretend, you know, to hold on to our jobs. But none of us is too excited about it all.

EMMA: I didn't want McKinley killed.

MATRON: We know that. You're standin' up for the boy, that's all.

(DISSOLVE TO: Emma in her cell, talking with a young lawyer.)

LAWYER: Czolgosz is insane. Darrow sent me to warn you that if you continue to deny that fact, no lawyer in the country will accept your defense.

EMMA: Why didn't Mr. Darrow come himself to warn me?

LAWYER: As you know, he's working to free the other anarchists arrested in the raids.

EMMA: I do know. Clarence Darrow is a man of broad social views. And of courage. And that is why he sent you in his stead. He knows the advice is reprehensible and can't bring himself to deliver it in person.

LAWYER: But Czolgosz *is* insane. Everyone says so.

EMMA: All I know is that the boy has been forsaken. I don't know his motives, and I don't know his state of mind. But I do know that he's been tortured enough to drive anyone insane.

LAWYER: I assure you, Miss Goldman, that unless you acknowledge Czolgosz's insanity, no prominent attorney can be found to defend your case.

EMMA: Then I'll defend my own. I will not swear away the reason and character of another human being—and one I don't even know.

LAWYER: Very well . . .

(As the lawyer rises to leave, DISSOLVE TO: Emma, being interviewed in her cell by reporters. Guards and detectives are standing by.)

FIRST REPORTER: Is it true that Hearst has offered you twenty-thousand dollars for an exclusive interview?

EMMA: Yes. (*smiling*) And I was tempted to accept it. We could have put that money to good use in the movement.

FIRST REPORTER: Have you accepted it?

EMMA: Hearst wants to railroad me in order to whitewash himself. His press has violently attacked President McKinley for months. Now he's loudest in demanding that all anarchists be exterminated.

FIRST REPORTER: Do you feel any personal animosity for the president?

EMMA: I think McKinley is the willing tool of Wall

Street and of the new American imperialism that's flowered under his administration with the annexation of the Philippines—an annexation directly contrary to his earlier pledge that he would set the islands free. But personal animosity toward him? No. In my professional capacity I would gladly nurse the president if asked to do so. I feel no personal dislike for the man. My sympathies, however, are with Czolgosz.

FIRST REPORTER: You're a puzzle, Emma Goldman. You sympathize with Czolgosz, yet you'd nurse the man he tried to kill.

EMMA: Reporters are supposed to understand human complexity. The boy is a creature at bay. Millions are ready to spring on him and tear him limb from limb. He committed his act for no personal reasons of gain. He did it for his ideal: what he calls the good of the people. That is why my sympathies are with him. On the other hand, William McKinley, suffering and probably near death, is also a human being. That is why I would nurse him.

(A reporter bursts into the cell.)

SECOND REPORTER: It's just come over the wire! McKinley is dead!

THIRD REPORTER: What are your feelings at this moment, Emma Goldman?

EMMA: Is it possible, gentlemen, that in the entire United States only the president passed away today? Surely many others have also died, most of them in poverty and destitution. Why do you expect me to feel more regret over the death of McKinley than over the deaths of the rest? My compassion has always been with the living; the dead no longer need it. Which is why most people are sympathetic toward them.

(The reporters start to dash out. One calls back:)

FOURTH REPORTER: I think you're crazy, Miss Goldman. But you're damned good copy!

(CUT TO: Emma, being transferred to a patrol wagon. Two handcuffed male prisoners are ahead of her. One has a bandage on his head. As they step into the van, the policeman pushes the first prisoner violently and clubs the bandaged one.)

EMMA: What are you doing, you brute?! These are helpless men, handcuffed and bandaged!

(CLOSE-UP—Emma's face just as the policeman's fist lands on her jaw. She's knocked to the ground, her face bloodied, a tooth knocked out. The officer stands above her menacingly.)

OFFICER: Another word from you, sister, and I'll break every bone in your body.

(FREEZE.)

(CUT TO: As Emma, blood still on her clothes and holding her jaw, walks down the corridor surrounded by police officers, a young child (voice-over) is heard:)

YOUNG CHILD *(voice-over):*   I am oh so sorry

That our President is dead
And everybody's sorry
So my father said
And the horrid man who killed him
Is a-sitting in his cell
And I'm glad that Emma Goldman
Doesn't board at this hotel.

(Emma and the officers have arrived in front of a door with RICHARD O'NEILL, CHIEF OF POLICE *lettered on it.)*

(CUT TO: Inside office.)

O'NEILL: Ah, Miss Goldman, I'm pleased to meet you at last. I want us to have a quiet talk.

EMMA: Having just had a tooth knocked out by one of your officers, talking may be difficult.

O'NEILL: The incident is much to be regretted. You have my apologies.

EMMA: Do I? Perhaps I might also have some water to wash. And a new tooth. And in exchange you're welcome to this souvenir. *(puts tooth down in front of him)* You might want to put it on display in a little velvet box, with a sign: The Day We Bagged Big Red Emma.

O'NEILL: We're going to set you free, Miss Goldman. I believe you're innocent of implication in the president's death.

EMMA: Did it take a month to discover that?

O'NEILL: We've now completed a detailed check on your activities in the six-month period prior to the assassination.

EMMA: My "activities" go back a good deal longer. And will go on a good deal longer, too.

O'NEILL: I advise you to stay out of the public eye for a time. The rest of the country doesn't seem to share my belief in your innocence. I must warn you that your life is in danger.

EMMA: That is what lives are for.

O'NEILL: There are friends waiting for you in the outer office. No further charges will be made.

(Emma rises, and picks up the tooth from the desk.)

EMMA: On second thought, I'll keep this myself. One needs some mementos in old age. Grandchildren love horror stories.

(FREEZE.)

(CUT TO: Emma with Anya and Brady. The mood is high spirited.)

ANYA: You're like a cat with nine lives, Emma; drop you out of a sixth-story window and you land on your paws.

BRADY *(offering a toast)*:   Here's to the gods who watch over Emma Goldman!

EMMA: They come in stranger form all the time. O'Neill would never have released me if it wasn't for the feud within the police department.

ANYA: I don't understand.

EMMA: O'Neill's enemies in the department were

trying to use my arrest to pose as saviors of the country—and thus win promotion over O'Neill's head. He was too shrewd for them—thank God!

(Laughter; a pause.)

EMMA: We must think what can be done for Czolgosz. Some effort has to be made in his behalf or he'll be gagged and railroaded just like Sasha before him. A mass meeting must be organized.

ANYA *(shaking her head sadly)*:   My dear, you're obviously not aware of the panic in the city. Not a hall in New York can be hired, and no one will speak out for Czolgosz.

EMMA *(angrily)*:   It is not a question of eulogizing his act. It is a matter of expressing sympathy for a doomed human being.

ANYA: No one seems up to that kind of bravery just now.

EMMA: We shall see.

(CUT TO: Emma, on the platform. Only a handful of people in the audience.)

EMMA: . . . The boy has been repeatedly beaten into unconsciousness. Notwithstanding all the torture, he's made no confession whatever and involved no one else in his act. Perhaps, in our mad world, that kind of integrity may well be considered the essence of sanity. . . .

(Emma's speech continues as voice-over during the MONTAGE of scenes below.)

EMMA *(voice-over)*: . . . Yes, I confess that in the past ten years, many doubts have assailed me about the utility and wisdom of political violence. I'm no longer sure that *any* means is justified, even when the end sought is human brotherhood. But I *am* as sure as ever that such acts are inevitable under existing conditions. I feel certain that behind every political deed of a violent nature, is an impressionable, highly sensitized, gentle spirit.

(During above: Czolgosz in the courtroom. He is half carried by guards to the dock. He is pale and emaciated, his head bandaged, his face swollen. His large, wistful eyes roam the courtroom, desperately searching for a friendly face. Finding none, he drops his gaze.)

EMMA *(voice-over)*: Such beings cannot go on living complacently, as most of us manage to do, in the sight of great human misery and wrong. Their sensitivity to cruelty finally expresses itself in cruelty, in some violent act that is a supreme rending of their tortured soul.

(CUT TO: Czolgosz being strapped into the electric chair. A black mask is placed over his face. The executioner stands with his hand on the switch, awaiting the signal.)

EMMA *(voice-over)*: So long as violence is employed by the rulers of our society, violence can be expected to be employed against them. McKinley, murdering thousands of Filipinos, is garlanded with honor. Czolgosz, murdering McKinley, is burned to death in the electric chair.

(The warden steps forward to Czolgosz, asks if he has any final word to say. Mumbled sounds from under the mask. The warden puts his ear closer to the slit covering Czolgosz's lips.)

CZOLGOSZ: . . . My act. Mine alone. I did for American people.

(The warden steps back and gives the signal to the executioner, who throws the switch. A sizzling sound. Czolgosz's body twitches.)

(CUT TO: Emma and Helena, sitting in the latter's living room in Rochester. They're holding hands.)

HELENA: I'm so glad you're here.

EMMA: New York isn't very hospitable to me just now. Many so-called "philosophical" anarchists turn out to be neither philosophers nor anarchists. Their belief in free speech has a remarkable number of "buts" attached to it. They deserted poor Czolgosz in droves. I thought the air might be a little cleaner here in Rochester.

HELENA: We've had a difficult time here too.

EMMA: You never wrote a word of that!

HELENA: Ah—you had enough . . .

EMMA: The beasts! Did they hurt the children?

HELENA: Stella was kept at police headquarters one whole day. They plied her with every kind of question. She refused to answer. All she would say was that she had pride and faith in her *tanta* Emma.

EMMA: God bless the child.

HELENA: Papa has suffered the most.

EMMA: You mean he *defended* me?

HELENA: Unwaveringly. He's changed a great deal, Emma. Much more patient and kindly. (*laughs.*) He denies he was ever any different!

EMMA: I won't refresh his memory.

HELENA: I'm glad. He's lost almost all his customers at the furniture store. None of his neighbors speak to him. They even excommunicated him from the synagogue.

EMMA: Poor old man. Maybe I'll see him before I go back.

HELENA: You will stay at least a few days?!

EMMA: Oh yes. I need to.

HELENA: Lena's oldest, Yegor, wants to return with you to New York. So does his chum, Dan. They insist they'll find an apartment for you *and* share the rent.

EMMA (*chuckling*):   I accept. I'm *eager* to be a docile female! How old is Dan?

HELENA: Nineteen. Very ardent, very handsome.

EMMA: Oh my—I hope he doesn't look too much like Sasha! I'm now, after all, an ancient thirty-two. Yes, I'd better have a talk with Papa.

(They laugh.)

HELENA: Some mail has been forwarded. I put it upstairs in your room.

(CUT TO: Emma, in her room, reading a letter from Berkman.)

BERKMAN *(voice-over)*:   "December 20, 1901. Dearest Girl: I lived in great fear for your safety, and I can barely credit the good news that you are at liberty. It seems almost a miracle. . . . You were splendid, dear. I was especially moved by your remark that you would faithfully nurse the wounded president. How impossible such a thought would have been to us a decade ago! It would have outraged all our traditions even to admit the humanity of an official representative of capitalism. We grow broader; but too often the heart contracts as the mind expands . . . the fires are burning down . . . you, dear friend . . . have yet happily kept your heart young."

(A knock on the door interrupts. Helena puts her head inside; she's carrying a tray.)

HELENA: I thought you might like some hot milk and butter before bed.

EMMA: Wonderful! I'm reading a letter from Sasha. It's the first in months. They put him in solitary again after McKinley was shot. I don't know how he stands it. I often feel I should be there, too. It isn't right somehow that I'm not. Only the lack of a few dollars prevented me from going with him to Pittsburg. It doesn't seem right.

HELENA: You've used your life well.

EMMA: I've *had* a life. What has Sasha had?

HELENA *(handing her the hot milk)*: What else does he say?

EMMA: He rejoices in how young I've stayed. *(laughs.)* Young? Ha! Not exactly Johann Most's "Little *blondkopf*" anymore! Hips like a hippopotamus. And no hourglass waist to go with the fashion! Ah, Helena, I miss Sasha. And Ed. And even the boy from the hotel room in St. Petersburg.

HELENA: Who?

EMMA: Never mind. Would you like to hear the rest of his letter?

HELENA: Oh yes!

(Emma starts reading again from Berkman's letter.)

EMMA: "Because I share your views in general it is the more distressing to disagree with you in one very important particular. I hope you will not mistake my expressed disagreement for condemnation."

(CLOSE-UP—Emma, startled.)

HELENA: He probably means your accepting a turkey dinner in jail.

EMMA *(continuing)*: "Czolgosz's deed represented the rebellion of a tortured soul. But the drastic measure of the deed must be resorted to only as a last extremity. (*stops, momentarily stunned; then continues in halting voice*) To prove of educational value, the deed must be motivated by social rather than individual necessity. This you may not understand, so I repeat: as an expression of personal revolt, Czolgosz's deed was inevitable, and in itself an indictment of existing conditions. But since the background of social necessity was lacking, the value of the act was to a great extent nullified." (*lets letter drop; rises in agitation*) What is he *saying*? How can Sasha of all people misunderstand?!

(*Helena picks up the letter and starts to scan it.*)

EMMA: Helena, I must be going crazy. No "social necessity"?! With millions brutalized in factories and war—no "social necessity"?!

HELENA: He explains, dear. Listen. Try to be calm. (*reading*) "McKinley could not be considered a direct enemy of the people, as in Russia, where the czar is absolute. Despotism is far more insidious here, because it rests on the popular delusion of self-government. That is the subtle source of democratic tyranny, and, as such, it cannot be reached with a bullet."

(*As Helena continues reading Berkman's letter, replay of earlier footage of Most declaring himself against Berkman's attack on Frick. Occasionally—at the indicated points—some of Most's actual words are heard above Helena's.*)

HELENA (*voice-over, reading*):   "In modern capitalism, exploitation rather than oppression is the real enemy of the people. Hence the battle is to be waged in the economic rather than the political field."

(Footage of Most addressing crowd.)

MOST: In a country like the United States, devoid of proletarian consciousness, individual acts of political violence are futile.

HELENA *(voice-over, reading)*: "I regard my own act as far more significant and educational than Czolgosz's. It was directed against a tangible oppressor, visualized as such by the people. As long as misery fills the world, our Czolgoszes will burst forth in rockets of iron. But does the lightning really illumine the social horizon, or merely confuse minds with the succeeding darkness?"

(During the above, we see the earlier footage of Emma, hysterical, approaching Most on the platform, brandishing the horse whip, and commencing to beat him. Emma breaks down into uncontrollable sobbing.)

EMMA *(to Helena, between sobs)*: Johann was my father . . . my teacher . . . the man I idolized . . . my father . . . my poor father . . . it's farce, Helena . . . it's all farce. . . .

(FREEZE.)

ACT THREE

(Emma, her nephew Yegor and his friend, Dan, are moving into a small apartment.)

EMMA: You and Dan take the back room, Yegor. I'll be comfortable here on the sofa.

DAN: No. The bedroom must be yours. Yegor and I can sleep out here.

YEGOR: Dan is right, Tanta.

EMMA: Well, we'll argue later. Let's get these boxes unpacked. *(looking around)* We'll make a home out of it—somehow.

(The downstairs buzzer rings. All three look concerned.)

EMMA: O'Neill promised no more harassment. Perhaps the politics of the police department have changed again.

YEGOR: I'll go.

(He exits. Emma looks concerned.)

DAN: Don't worry. You have us to protect you.

EMMA: Thank you, Dan. It's good to have two strong men about.

(Yegor comes back into the room, bearing a calling card.)

YEGOR: It's someone named Garson.

EMMA: Garson! It can't be! *(takes the card, reads it)* "I would consider it an honor if you would allow me an audience at once. The matter is urgent." (*almost to herself*) Indeed all is farce.

DAN: Is he safe?

EMMA: My first job in this country was sewing overcoat belts in Mr. Garson's "model factory." I quit when he wouldn't raise my salary above two fifty a week. No, he's not "safe," Dan. He's a criminal. But not the kind that's ever punished.

YEGOR: Do you need me here?

EMMA: No, dear.

YEGOR: I want to get some nails and a hammer from the corner store.

EMMA: We'll be fine. Just show Mr. Garson up.

(*Yegor exits. CLOSE-UP—Emma, as she plumps herself down regally on top of one of the boxes, and folds her arms across her chest. Dan looks at her in some bewilderment.*)

(*CLOSE-UP—Garson entering, his hat humbly in his hand.*)

GARSON: Miss Goldman—what a wonderful pleasure after all these years.

EMMA: It *has* been a long time, Mr. Garson. I'm afraid this is no match for your luxurious office. I can at least offer you a seat—which is more, I recall, than you once did for me.

(*Dan brings over a box and Garson awkwardly sits himself on it.*)

GARSON: You've become a famous woman. I can hardly believe that the little seamstress who I—

EMMA: —who you were so rude to, might after all, have had something to say worth listening to. Now then: What can I do for you? As you see, we are busy establishing a home.

GARSON: Why nothing at all, dear Miss Goldman. I only wanted the pleasure of a chat.

EMMA: I see.

(Emma folds her arms and waits. Garson squirms.)

GARSON: As you know, Miss Goldman, I've worked hard all my life, saving penny by penny, putting in hours longer than any of my factory hands.

EMMA: Very few of your "hands," as you put it, have been able to save "penny by penny."

GARSON: They all made good livings.

EMMA: Strange, then, that none has been able to open a factory of his own.

GARSON: As you know, many are ignorant and extravagant.

EMMA: You used those same words to me long ago—in reference to my wanting to buy an occasional book. I stood like a beggar before you, asking for a raise of a dollar a week.

GARSON: You've become a grand speaker—just as everyone says.

EMMA: And can that possibly have something to do with your visit?

GARSON *(embarrassed):*   Well as you know, Miss Goldman, times are hard, and I've had heavy losses. The workers don't seem to understand that profits are not what they were. They've gone on strike, and I thought you perhaps . . . since I gave you your first job in this country . . . that you perhaps could explain to them the truth of economic conditions.

EMMA: If I could get them to see the "truth of economic conditions," Mr. Garson, they would close your plant down permanently, and assume the ownership for themselves.

GARSON: I've heard you've had hard times, what with the public outcry against you after the president's death. I love giving beautiful women beautiful presents. Some say it's my old-fashioned side, I'm—

(Emma laughs out loud.)

EMMA: They're right, Mr. Garson. You're remarkably old-fashioned. It's what makes me laugh—instead of spit.

GARSON: Come now, Miss Goldman, there's no cause for—

EMMA *(rising):*   —Good day, Mr. Garson. The interview is over.

(Garson, in a huff, starts to leave.)

EMMA: Just a moment. Don't forget your silk hat.

If my friends found it here, it would cause a terrible scandal.

(Garson grabs his hat and exits.)

EMMA: Idiot!

(CLOSE-UP—Dan's face, shining with admiration.)

DAN: You were fine, Emma, amazingly fine.

EMMA *(laughs):* He should be shaken to his boots. Yet somehow I'm amused. A sign, I suppose, that I'm getting older.

DAN *(going up to her):* Emma, you're the youngest woman I've ever known. All the others are stupid. They have nothing to say or give.

EMMA: Well, I *am* a talker.

(Dan tentatively puts his arm around her.)

DAN: And a giver?

EMMA: I . . . I don't know, Dan . . .

(He bends down and kisses her on the lips, first tentatively, then as she responds, passionately. FREEZE.)

(CUT TO: Emma, dressed in her nurse's uniform, and a young man [Robert], conferring in hushed tones outside a patient's door.)

ROBERT: Mother's found out who you are, Emma. She knows you're not Nurse Smith.

EMMA *(resigned):* Well, I guess that's that. At least I got three weeks' work out of it. Thanks for covering for me, Robert. Work's been hard to find.

(A woman's voice calls out from the inner room.)

WOMAN: Robert! Miss Goldman! I can hear you. Come in here.

(They enter the room.)

WOMAN *(to Emma):* Did he tell you all the terrible things I've said about you?

EMMA: No—only that you threatened to soak me in kerosene and burn me alive if the president died.

WOMAN *(to Robert):* How could you repeat such vicious things?

ROBERT: But you did say them, Mother!

WOMAN: That was before I knew Miss Goldman. Before she nursed me so well. *(to Emma)* I've discharged the day nurse. I want you to take her place. *(takes Emma's hand)* Such a wonderful nurse!

(FREEZE.)

(CUT TO: Ed Brady and Emma in her apartment. The floor is strewn with boxes. Brady is opening up the last one.)

BRADY: And now, the piece de résistance!

(He takes out a coat with an astrakhan collar, muff, and turban to match.)

EMMA: Oh Ed, how beautiful! But it isn't right for me to take such expensive gifts. What about your family?

BRADY: S-sh! It's Christmas! And I'm getting rich. Besides, this is the way I've always wanted my Emma to look.

(She tries on the coat. It's the same one she wore in scene one, the Buford*).*

EMMA: Maybe someday everyone will have such beautiful things.

BRADY: Emma, come look.

(CLOSE-UP: Snapshot; Brady holds picture of three-year-old girl.)

EMMA: Your daughter! How big she's getting! And what a beautiful face. Why do you never bring her to see me?

BRADY: Why? The mother! The mother! If you only knew the mother.

EMMA: S-sh, please. Don't let's talk about her. I don't want to know more.

BRADY: You should know more. It was my rage against you that drove me to her. I was maddened by your loss. I even took to drink—for months—to blot out the resentment.

147 • • •

EMMA: Oh Ed, not resentment?

BRADY: Yes, yes, resentment! Even hatred—that you could give up our love so easily.

EMMA: I loved you. But you wouldn't let me *be*.

BRADY: When the child was born, I wanted to wrap her up and come to you, to beg you to start again. But I was too proud. And you were too busy. The marriage is finished, Emma. It would have broken even if you and I had never become friends again.

EMMA: The past is done. Don't rake it up.

BRADY: You have to listen! *(turning quiet and serious.)* Emma: Come to Europe with me. I have the means now. We can take the child. Just travel and enjoy ourselves, for months and months.

EMMA: Take the child? But what about her mother? It's her child, too. You can't rob her of it.

BRADY *(taking Emma's face in his hands)*: You're the one who's always talked against "mother love"—against suffocating a child.

EMMA: I know, I know. Just the same, the woman endures the agony of birth. She nourishes the infant with her substance. Can't you see how unjust it would be, Ed? Go to Europe with you? I'd do it in a minute! But I can't rob a mother of her child.

(Brady stands up. He's quietly furious.)

BRADY: You're like all of them. Advanced ideas, but in practice traditional. You rail against men for all the wrongs they do women, but never see what the man suffers. I'll go to Europe with my little girl. Alone.

(He takes his hat and walks out. FREEZE.)

(CUT TO: Emma, dressed in her nurse's uniform, approaching the doorway to her building, late at night. A friend [Claus] is standing there waiting for her.)

EMMA: Claus! What are you doing here at such an hour?

CLAUS: I have bad news, Emma. It's about Ed.

EMMA: Ed? You have a message from Ed?

CLAUS: No more messages, Emma. Ed . . . Ed died earlier this evening.

EMMA: You're drunk! Ed can't be dead! He can't be!

(Claus gently pulls her to him.)

CLAUS: It must have been a heart attack. He got sick in a bar, fell, and hit his head. They got him into a cab. But he never regained consciousness.

EMMA *(moaning)*:   Ed . . . oh, no . . . not Ed . . .

(CUT TO: Door of the funeral parlor. Emma is arguing with Claus.)

EMMA: I *will* see Ed again. I *will!*

CLAUS: She's sworn to keep you out. It can only be an ugly scene. She keeps repeating that you robbed her of Ed when he was alive, but you won't rob her in death.

EMMA: The ceremony's been over for hours. No one will be there. I must see Ed again.

(Emma pushes her way past Claus into the funeral parlor.)

(CUT TO: Interior of parlor. CLOSE-UP —The closed coffin. Claus lifts the cover. Emma looks in and starts to cry.)

EMMA: Oh, the dear face . . . the dear face . . .

(A piercing scream from the back of the funeral parlor.)

MRS. BRADY *(hysterical)*: My husband! My husband! He's mine! He's mine!

(CLOSE-UP—The shrieking Mrs. Brady rushing to throw herself between Emma and the coffin. When she reaches Emma, she roughly pushes her aside.)

(CLOSE-UP—A little girl—the one from the photograph—sobbing, and with frightened eyes, clutching at her mother's dress.)

(CLOSE-UP—Emma, rushing out.)

(CUT TO: Emma in her room, writing to Berkman.)

EMMA *(voice-over)*: Sasha dear, It wasn't only the finality of Ed's death that tore me apart. It had been years, after all, since we've been lovers. But it made me look so deep into myself, brought back so many memories . . .

(As Emma continues voice-over, CUT TO: MONTAGE of her boarding a train, sitting alone in a railroad car, staring sadly out of the window, arriving at a depot, carrying her luggage to a hansom cab, entering a public hall.)

EMMA *(voice-over)*:   I seem always torn between my hunger for love and my inability to have it for long. Is it me? Some passionate yearning that no man can ever fulfill? Or is it common to all of us who put a public ideal ahead of private satisfaction? Perhaps it's the inevitable price we pay: occasional snatches of love, but nothing permanent except an ideal. But this is self-pity. I *must* plunge back into work, make my life count for more than a round of personal concerns. The radical community is coming back to life again after news of the pogroms in Russia, and the widespread labor strikes beginning here. I must stop nursing and take up the Cause with new strength. I have invitations for a lecture tour. The striking garment workers in Rochester have invited me. And the coal miners in Pennsylvania. I will go—I must . . . Only think, Sasha dear, less than thirty months now, and I will be able to hold you next to my heart. . . . We have survived so much. . . .

(CUT TO: Emma, on the platform. She's pointing at two figures seated in the front row.)

EMMA: . . . That's Grandpa Jones. He's ninety and he's worked in the mines for seventy years. Next to him sits his great-grandchild. They say he's fourteen, but in fact he's *eight*. A man of ninety and a child of eight working side by side ten hours a day in a black pit. Perhaps that is what our rulers mean by "a land of equal opportunity"!

(CUT TO: Emma sitting exhausted on a cot in a miner's cabin. Three children are crowded into a single folding bed. A baby wails continually in the background. The mother hands Emma a glass of milk.)

MOTHER: This should help. It's nice and warm.

EMMA: Oh thank you. I'm so parched. *(drinks milk)*

MOTHER: That should make you sleep.

EMMA: Why does the baby cry so? Is she ill?

MOTHER *(evasive)*:   My breast milk is poor. She must be bottle fed.

EMMA: You don't mean, you gave me the *baby's* bottle?!

MOTHER *(guiltily)*:   Baby had one bottle earlier. You looked so tired and you coughed. What else could I do?

(CLOSE-UP—Emma, putting her hands over her eyes as she starts to cry.)

(CUT TO: Emma, on the platform.)

EMMA: . . . One cannot adequately appreciate social unrest simply by reading the literature of propaganda. We must also become conversant with the larger phrases of human expression manifest in art, literature, and, above all, the modern drama. The works of Gorky, Hauptmann, Shaw, and Ibsen have not only disseminated radical thought but have given it its most deeply felt expression. Above all, I want to speak of the work of Henrik Ibsen.

(A police sergeant jumps up to the platform.)

SERGEANT: You're not sticking to the terms of the permit, Miss Goldman. If you don't stick to the agreed-on subject, we'll stop the meeting.

EMMA: I *am* sticking to my subject!

SERGEANT: Nothing of the kind! Your subject is the modern drama. And you're talking about some radical name *Ibsen!*

(FREEZE.)

(CUT TO: A crowded apartment. Emma is being introduced to a man and a woman [Orleneff and Nazimova]. Dan is with her.)

EMMA: A great honor, Pavel Orleneff, Madame Nazimova. Friends took me to see your marvelous production of *The Chosen People.* I have never seen such ensemble work, such deeply felt emotion. No play could be a greater protest against the pogroms in Russia.

ORLENEFF: That is why we bring it to America. But your people no come! Have great company. But no great *publika*—how you say in English?

EMMA: Audience.

ORLENEFF: You know that word? You be my manager!

EMMA: Your manager?! Pavel Orleneff, it's a great honor, but I have no experience in such matters.

ORLENEFF: You like Orleneff? Like Nazimova?

EMMA: Yes.

ORLENEFF: Then you have experience.

DAN: Oh do it, Emma—it'll be fun. And you've got no lectures planned all summer.

NAZIMOVA: Ah yes, please, Madame Goldman. No friends. No money. No English. Must help artists.

DAN: We have an island—all to ourselves!

ORLENEFF: High land? What is for "High Land"?

EMMA: Island: *ostrov*. We couldn't afford a vacation. So we've pitched a tent on Hunter's Island in Pelham Bay.

DAN: Not only that, but we got *legal* permission to do it!

EMMA: We can pitch another tent for you and your troupe—though God knows if we'll all survive.

NAZIMOVA: *Je ne comprend.* Too fast.

ORLENEFF *(explaining to Nazimova):* Tent. The steppes, *Tartari, Kossaki* . . .

NAZIMOVA: *Kossaki?! Oi, gospodi!* . . . *(keels over in a dead faint)*

(DISSOLVE TO: Hunter's Island. A huge bonfire. Orleneff is in the center, guitar in hand, softly strumming to the accompaniment of his own singing. The whole troupe joins in on the chorus.)

(CLOSE-UP—Emma, tending a huge samovar, pouring coffee, at the same time joining in the singing.)

(CLOSE-UP—Nazimova, taking Emma aside. Dan follows. Nazimova mimes the buzzing of mosquitos, then shows Emma the painful bumps on her arms and legs. Dan runs off and comes back with some ointment. He applies it gently to the bitten areas. Nazimova sighs with pleasure. Emma, half-amused, half-jealous, goes back to the samovar.)

(CUT TO: The office of Arthur Hornblow, editor of Theatre Magazine.)

HORNBLOW: Miss Smith, allow me to present Mr. Harrison Grey Fiske, and his wife, Minnie Maddern Fiske.

EMMA ["Miss Smith"]: I'm honored. Your performances, Mrs. Fiske, are among my treasured moments in the theater.

MRS. FISKE: Thank you, Miss Smith. That's very kind. We understand you're managing the Orleneff troupe.

EMMA: In a manner of speaking. I'm really only a friend trying to help. I don't have your experience in theatrical matters, Mr. Fiske.

FISKE: How lucky for you! Nothing ever happens the same way twice in the theater. Experience is just another name for tenacity.

EMMA: Then Orleneff may be right: I do have experience.

MRS. FISKE: Mr. Hornblow tells us the troupe has fallen on difficult times. We can't understand it. We went ourselves to see them at the Third Street Theater. Orleneff was superb as Nachman. And the place was packed. Every critic and writer in New York seemed to be there.

FISKE: And the few actors who dared, like John and Ethel Barrymore.

EMMA: We rebuilt that theatre ourselves, going back and forth from our island. Actually, it was nice to get away from the mosquitos and poison ivy.

HORNBLOW: We've run several pieces on the troupe in *Theatre Magazine*. But still their audiences have dwindled to nothing.

MRS. FISKE: I can't understand it.

EMMA: It's the failure of the October Revolution in Russia. Now that the massacre of Jews has started again, everything Russian is being boycotted. A vicious rumor's even been spread that some of Orleneff's troupe are members of the

Black Hundred, the Russian Jew-baiters. Absurd, but there it is.

FISKE: How can we help?

EMMA: We want to organize a benefit performance to raise money. Some of the troupe wants to go home; probably Orleneff among them. Nazimova wants to stay in America and prepare herself for the English stage. In short, we need sponsors.

MRS. FISKE: Put us first on your list.

FISKE: And we'll get others for you, too, Miss Smith.

(Hornblow signals Fiske that he needs a private word with him.)

FISKE: Excuse me for a moment.

(He and Hornblow confer to the side.)

MRS. FISKE: I hope you at least get a decent salary for all your trouble, Miss Smith.

EMMA: Orleneff has urged one on me, but no— there's not enough money. As it is, Nazimova makes all the costumes herself by hand. If you've seen the court dresses for *Tsar Feodor*, you can imagine the labor!

MRS. FISKE: But how do you live yourself?

EMMA: Oh . . . odd jobs. You know. I sew. And do some nursing.

MRS. FISKE: Harrison would never stand for that.

He'd regard an unsalaried manager as a crime against nature.

FISKE *(bellowing, as he strides toward Emma):* *Emma Goldman,* aren't you ashamed of yourself?!

HORNBLOW: I felt I had to tell him, Emma, if they're to be sponsors.

EMMA: I apologize. I hate deception. But otherwise every door would have been closed. And I had to think first of Orleneff.

FISKE: Not *every* door. "Miss Smith" indeed! Emma Goldman—that's the girl! Now shake, and don't ever doubt us again!

(FREEZE. CUT TO: Backstage, after the benefit. The last people are leaving the dressing room. Only Orleneff and Emma remain. They embrace.)

ORLENEFF: So. Not a big "aud-i-ence," eh? But enough, enough to get home to *Matushka Rossiya.* And to you, Emma, I owe all. *(embraces her again)* And now: *my* surprise. Please: Close eyes, and hold out hands.

EMMA: Pavel, what in the—

ORLENEFF: —S-sh. Do as the czar commands!

(Emma closes her eyes and opens her hands. CLOSE-UP—Her hands, as Orleneff fills them with money.)

EMMA: Pavel! What is this?!

ORLENEFF: Two hundred and fifty dollar! Your share. To start your magazine. *(she hugs him)* You see, I no forget. Once I ask you what you most want if you have money. Now you have money. Now magazine. Spread great truths. *(Emma starts to cry)* Now, now, if you cry so well you steal Nazimova part in *Countess Julia!* *(Emma laughs.)* And I have name for magazine, too. *Mother Earth*. It is our Emma.

(They hug again.)

EMMA *(softly)*: Pavel, I want to share something with you, too. All on one day. I can't believe it. My *last* letter from Sasha. In two weeks he'll be free. And now the magazine, too. *(she starts to weep again)*

ORLENEFF: S-sh! Read letter.

(CLOSE-UP—Emma, as she dries her eyes and starts to read.)

EMMA: "Dearest Girl: It's Wednesday morning, the nineteenth, at last! Geh stiller, meines Herzens Schlag Und schliesst euch alle meine alten Wunden, Denn dieses ist mein letzter fag, Und dies sind seine letzten Stunden! My last thoughts within these walls are of you, dear friend, the Immutable. Sasha." But Pavel—you don't know German, do you?!

ORLENEFF: German, English—what matter. I hear your feeling.

(CLOSE-UP—Emma's vibrant face as she translates the poem into English.)

159 •••

EMMA: Go slower, beating heart of mine
And close, ye bleeding wounds
This is my final day
And these its waning hours.

(FREEZE. When Emma's face reanimates, she is standing on a railroad platform waiting for the train bearing Berkman to come to a stop. She has a bouquet of roses in one hand. Her other hand is around a pillar, holding onto it for dear life. CLOSE-UP—Train, as it stops. Several people get off. Then, Berkman. He has on an ill-fitting suit and an incongruous summer straw hat. He looks bewildered, almost paralyzed. As the crowd clears away, the line of vision to Emma is open. Berkman sees her and starts toward her. Emma doesn't move; she continues to hold on to the pillar.)

(CLOSE-UP—Emma's face, terror stricken. Berkman throws his arms around her. They stand in an embrace, barely moving, saying nothing. Emma brushes the tears from her eyes and silently hands Berkman the roses. He holds the flowers to his face, and mechanically bites the petals.)

(CUT TO: Grave of Haymarket martyrs at Waldheim cemetery, as Berkman lays the wreath of roses. Then he and Emma stand silently in front of the monument, arm in arm. Sounds of footsteps, running toward them. A young woman [Alice] appears, her face flushed with excitement.)

(CLOSE-UP—Emma's face, slightly annoyed.)

(CLOSE-UP—Berkman, frightened.)

ALICE: I knew you'd be here! I told them it would be your first stop.

EMMA: Sasha, this is Alice. She is working with us on *Mother Earth*.

(Berkman mumbles an inaudible greeting.)

ALICE: They're frantic at the reception! They thought maybe something went wrong at the last minute.

BERKMAN *(frightened)*:   Reception?

EMMA *(soothingly)*:   Only a few friends, dear. At my apartment. They insisted they had to welcome you.

ALICE: Oh, Mr. Berkman, it's such an honor. . . . You and Johann Most have always been—

EMMA *(interrupting)*:   —Alice, be calm, dear, be calm.

BERKMAN *(almost somnambulant)*:   Most is dead. Most is dead.

EMMA: You know, then?

BERKMAN: They told me you spoke at the memorial meeting.

EMMA: Yes, dear. I felt I owed it to the early years.

BERKMAN *(quietly)*:   Yes, the early years . . . the early years . . .

(DISSOLVE TO: Emma, Alice, and Berkman, crossing the street. Berkman clings to Emma. He seems terrified of the noises, the turmoil. As a horseless

161 •••

carriage goes by, he stops dead in his tracks and stares at it incredulously.)

EMMA: An automobile, dear. An automobile.

BERKMAN *(mechanically repeating)*:   Automobile . . . Everyone is staring. . . . Why is everyone staring at me?

ALICE: It's only that it's early in the season for a boater, Mr. Berkman. Oh, they're very fashionable, they really are. But in February a derby, a nice dark derby, would be better.

(They are passing a hat store.)

ALICE: We could go in right here. I'll do it for you! If you give me the hat size, I'll—

(She makes a tentative motion as if to reach for Berkman's boater. He draws back in horror.)

EMMA: It might be more comfortable, dear.

BERKMAN: My head. They shaved my head. The last minute, they shaved my head.

(He looks as if he might break down, but manages to control himself.)

BERKMAN: Two hundred prisoners asked the warden if I could pass along the tiers to say goodbye. He said no. Then they shaved my head.

(Again he looks as if he might cry. CLOSE-UP— Emma, as she puts her arm around him.)

(FREEZE.)

(CUT TO: Emma and Berkman alone in her apartment. Berkman is wearing a skull cap instead of the boater. He rubs his hands along the paper on the wall, caressing it over and over.)

BERKMAN: So soft . . . so soft . . .

EMMA: Come sit down, dear.

(Berkman slowly goes over to her on the couch. Along the way he picks up a piece of bric-a-brac from the table. After sitting next to Emma, he continues to fondle the piece and stare at it.)

EMMA: It's a little toy. Undine, rising from the water. See how the spray glistens when you hold it to the light. Alice bought it for me. She's such a sweet girl. And works so hard for the magazine.

BERKMAN: All those others. I hardly knew a face. And Fedya? Where is Fedya?

EMMA: We don't see him now. He's doing well. He illustrates for a big magazine. He never turned his back, dear. Just slowly drifted away. You know.

BERKMAN: The new ones talk so much. I can't talk . . . yet.

EMMA: They were excited. They worked so hard raising the five hundred dollars for you. They said they *had* to present it on your first day.

BERKMAN: It isn't right. . . . All those left behind in prison . . . they wouldn't let me say good-

bye,   Emma . . . no   good-byes . . . no
good-byes . . .

*(He breaks down in fierce sobs, burying his head in
Emma's lap.)*

(FREEZE.)

*(JUMP CUT: Emma's apartment. She, Alice, and
one or two other helpers are working on the magazine. Various layouts on the floor.)*

*(Berkman is slumped on the couch, taking no part.
Emma holds up the cover of the magazine with
Mother Earth written on it in bold letters.)*

EMMA: What do you think, Sasha? Does it catch
the eye?

BERKMAN *(perfunctorily):*   Yes. Are there more
blintzes? The meat ones, the ones with meat?

EMMA: Dearest, you ate two dozen at breakfast!

BERKMAN: They're to eat, they're to eat! If you didn't
want me to eat them, why did you make them?

(Emma quickly puts down the poster.)

EMMA: I'll cook more. I've got batter for a hundred.

BERKMAN *(jumping up):*   Don't mother me. I'm not
a sick child. *(pause)* This is absurd. You have
important work to do. Or so you seem to believe.
(starts to leave)

EMMA: Sasha, you know how much the magazine
means to—

BERKMAN: —words, words! What have they to do with revolution? Another little essay on Ibsen maybe, and the "creative force of modern drama." Soon the society ladies will be giving teas for you, and you can shock them with your "advanced ideas."

EMMA: It's *you* who denounced Czolgosz!

BERKMAN: *My* deed mattered! It increased the people's understanding!

(Emma goes toward him, as if to embrace him.)

EMMA: Please, Sasha, don't let's quarrel. No one knows what to do. We do what we can.

(CLOSE-UP—Berkman, as he roughly pushes her away and starts toward the door.)

BERKMAN: Do nothing. For you that would be a positive change.

(As he exits, DISSOLVE TO: Berkman, sitting in a bar. Two prostitutes, one middle-aged, one young, are at his table. All three are drunk.)

(CLOSE-UP—Older prostitute, as she pokes Berkman.)

OLDER PROSTITUTE: Now listen, you, she wrote them poems herself. Let's have a little respect, eh? *(to younger prostitute)* Read 'im the other, dear. *(pokes Berkman again)* Ah, here's the one; brings tears to me eyes every time.

YOUNGER PROSTITUTE *(to Berkman, timidly)*:   You're sure   you   like   poetry?

(He doesn't answer.)

OLDER PROSTITUTE: *I* like poetry! *Read.*

YOUNGER PROSTITUTE: Mother dear, the days were
young
When posies in our garden
hung.
Upon your lap my golden
head I laid,
With pure and happy heart I
prayed.

OLDER PROSTITUTE *(teary)*:   Sure and don't we all
remember such happy things? Our laps on
Mummsie's golden hair.

(FREEZE.)

*(CUT TO: Berkman, lying on a cot in a filthy hotel
room. He's staring vacantly at the ceiling. Loud
knocking at door. It repeats.)*

VOICE: Mister? Hey—mister?!

BERKMAN: Yes.

VOICE: You all right in there?

BERKMAN: Yes.

VOICE: You ain't been out of your room in two
days.

BERKMAN: No, in fourteen years.

VOICE: What say?

(Berkman doesn't answer.)

VOICE *(receding)*:   Well, you got to Wednesday to rot. Rent's due at noon Wednesday.

(DISSOLVE TO: Emma's apartment. She's arguing with Claus. Alice is also there.)

EMMA: I know I promised two weeks ago! Max will speak in my place. Or Yegor. Get someone, anyone.

CLAUS: It's you they want to hear.

EMMA: Well they *can't*! I'm tired of all the words, tired of them!

ALICE *(comforting her)*:   He'll come back, Emma. I know he will.

EMMA *(quietly)*:   Why would he? Why stand by the wreckage of a life.

ALICE: But he's still a young man! Not yet forty!

EMMA: I meant my life.

(FREEZE.)

(CUT TO: Street, in front of the apartment. Berkman is huddled in a doorway, staring up at the building. He removes a gun from his pocket, closes his eyes, and puts it to his head. His hand trembles. A moment passes. He brings his hand down. He moves out of the doorway and away from the street.)

(CUT TO: Berkman in a telegraph office, haggard,

pale. ZOOM to the message he's writing out on the pad: "I must see you once more. Come. I am waiting for you here.")

(CUT TO: Emma running full speed down the street. The CAMERA PICKS UP Berkman's form ahead of her; he's against a wall, barely standing.)

(CLOSE-UP—Emma holding him to her. She's crying.)

EMMA *(over and over)*:   Oh, my dear . . . oh my dear . . .

(CUT TO: Emma's apartment. CLOSE-UP—Berkman in bed. He opens his eyes. Emma's figure appears over him.)

EMMA: Awake, dearest?

BERKMAN: Yes. When did I come here?

EMMA: Two days ago. You've been very sick.

BERKMAN: Where was I before?

EMMA *(stammering)*:   You . . . you were . . . absent.

(JUMP CUT TO: Emma, carrying a large bowl of soup on a tray. Alice is about to open the door for her to Berkman's bedroom. Suddenly Emma stops. Alice looks at her quizzically.)

ALICE: Something wrong?

EMMA: You take the soup to him. You take it. Yes, yes—*you.*

ALICE: I don't understand, Emma.

EMMA *(almost to herself)*:   The years in between—he's never had them. He needs . . . he needs to be twenty-one.

(As Alice disappears through the bedroom door with the soup, CLOSE-UP—Emma's face, melancholy.)

EMMA *(barely audible)*:   Sachs's Café. I wonder what has happened to Sachs's Café. . . .

(She puts her head in her hands and starts to cry.)

(CUT TO: Berkman's bedside. He is talking to a friend.)

FRIEND: Life is a problem. A problem whose solution consists in trying to solve it. We can only try for a little more harmony, a few more possibilities. . . .

BERKMAN: But everything is so different from what I remembered. Our comrades, the movement—it's not as it was.

FRIEND: I know what you miss, dear Sasha: the old sense that we were living on the very threshold of the revolution. That *tomorrow*, the world would be new.

BERKMAN: Everything is strange.

FRIEND: Stay longer. You'll see that only the form has changed. The essence is the same. Even in this country, there's an awakening. A new ferment.

(Emma enters the room.)

EMMA: Are you crooning Sasha to sleep?

BERKMAN: No, I'm wide awake.

FRIEND: It's getting late. I have to be off to the meeting.

BERKMAN: What meeting?

FRIEND: To protest the new Criminal Anarchy Law deporting anyone opposed to the "patriotic struggle" against Germany.

BERKMAN: I think—I'd like to come along.

(Emma moves toward him eagerly.)

BERKMAN: I think, dear, Alice knows where my boater is. Ask her if she can find it, will you? *(feels the top of his head)* Maybe I won't need it. My hair's growing in a little.

(FREEZE.)

(CUT TO: Emma, on the platform. Berkman and Alice are sitting in the front row of the auditorium, holding hands.)

EMMA: . . . As a woman, not subject to military service, I can't advise people on refusing to serve in the armed forces. Whether or not one lends oneself to the killing should be left to the individual conscience. An anarchist can't presume to decide the fate of others. But I do support the No-Conscription League. And I say to those who refuse to be coerced into military service that I will plead their cause and stand by their act anywhere. *(loud applause)* It is now my great pleasure to introduce to you one of the guiding spirits of the No-Conscription League: Alexander Berkman.

(CUT TO: Berkman rising and coming up on the platform.)

BERKMAN *(hesitantly)*:   As you know, I've only recently been released from fourteen years in prison. . . . I'm not used to talking much. . . .

(Encouraging applause from the audience. CLOSE-UP—Emma's face, full of concern.)

BERKMAN: But I want to say that life in prison is like in an army. Both are designed to destroy human feeling . . . though somehow the feeling struggles to survive. . . .

(CLOSE-UP—Berkman's face, panicky. He turns to Emma. She comes up on the platform to stand by him. He continues.)

BERKMAN: As war fever spreads in Europe . . . sparks are catching fire here. More and more we hear the need for "preparedness." Preparedness for what? For murder. Many of our socialist comrades are joining in saying we must take sides with the Allies. But what are they allied for? To maintain the old world as it is. In this they are exactly the same as the Prussians they oppose. All are concerned with maintaining governments that serve the interests of the few at the expense of the many. And to achieve that, they are happy to let the many get killed. Those who hope for a new world have nothing to gain by defending either side in this struggle. And they have everything to lose. The international movement against the rule of the plutocrats will be wrecked if the workers of any country put nationalist fervor above the interests of the masses of people everywhere. *(loud applause)* I think . . . I think that's all I care to say for now. . . .

(Cheers from the audience. Emma embraces Berkman on the platform.)

(DISSOLVE TO: An empty storefront. Berkman, Alice, and Emma are conferring with Ben Reitman, a florid, exotic figure. Wearing a large black cowboy hat and flowing silk tie, and carrying a huge cane, he exudes animal vitality and an irrepressible, childlike spirit. He has a handsome head, large dreamy eyes, a mass of black, dirty, curly hair.)

REITMAN: The hell with the authorities! They said you *could* speak, right?

EMMA: If *I* find a place. But not a hall in town will rent to us.

(Reitman makes a sweeping gesture behind him to the empty storefront.)

REITMAN: Here, my dear Miss Goldman, you see your hall. *(suddenly inspired)* No—better still! We hire an automobile and tour the city in it, the two of you talking from the back seat! We make it a circus performance! Everywhere photographers, flash lights—maybe even dancing girls to pave the way at each stop!

BERKMAN *(cold)*: We are not a circus, Mr. Reitman.

REITMAN: We have to make the venture *hum*! If P. T. Barnum can get 'em for elephants, we can get 'em for Emma Goldman! (*he catches himself and bows low in apology to Emma*) Forgive me, my dear Emma Goldman.

EMMA *(laughs)*: I've been compared to much worse, Mr. Reitman. In fact, the analogy is apt: Both our skins are tough.

ALICE: Emma won't be speaking alone, Mr. Reitman.

REITMAN: Of course not. We will *all* be speaking!

BERKMAN: The automobile is impossible. I'll have no part of it.

EMMA: I entirely agree with Sasha. It would vulgarize our effort. (*starts to inspect the store front*) And frankly, Mr. Reitman, this doesn't look much more promising.

REITMAN: With my hobos, we'll have it cleaned up in three days.

BERKMAN: With your what?

REITMAN: Hobos. Ben Reitman is King of the Hobos. Every outcast in the city comes to me with his troubles. I have a deep feeling for derelicts. Which is why I sought you out.

(CLOSE-UP—Berkman's astonished face.)

(DISSOLVE TO: A group of hobos hard at work cleaning up the store, Reitman directing activities. Platforms are being built, benches arranged. Emma, Alice, and some of the women are sewing material for curtains.)

(CLOSE-UP— Fire department official striding into the store. Reitman goes right up to him.)

REITMAN: Inspector Holliday, welcome to our new church!

HOLLIDAY: Church, is it?

REITMAN: Got to give the poor things faith, something to live for.

HOLLIDAY: And who'll be doin' the preaching?

REITMAN: Whoever the spirit moves, praised be God!

HOLLIDAY: We've had word Emma Goldman is to speak.

REITMAN: Any poor sinner who feels the call, Inspector—as our own dear Lord might have said.

HOLLIDAY: If Goldman speaks, the meeting's over. We stop it on a dime. Don't say you weren't warned, Reitman.

REITMAN: Much obliged, Inspector. Hope to see you in person tonight. Who knows through what strange vessel Jesus might make himself felt.

(Holliday exits. CLOSE-UP—Reitman, in thought. Emma comes up to him.)

EMMA: Trouble?

REITMAN: Opportunity *(takes her aside)* Come, Emma, I have a little plan to confide.

(JUMP CUT TO—Berkman, coming into the store carrying a newspaper. He's scowling angrily. He comes up to Reitman and Emma, brandishing the paper.)

BERKMAN: Reitman: Are you responsible for this?

(Reitman takes the paper. CLOSE-UP—His face, grinning broadly.)

REITMAN: My God—the front page! Not even Barnum could have managed it.

BERKMAN *(to Emma)*:   The papers are full of stories that you and I are planning to blow up the American fleet now in the harbor!

EMMA: The *whole* fleet?!

BERKMAN: It's a ridiculous invention. Degrading to our purpose.

(He stalks off.)

(DISSOLVE TO: Berkman and several others sitting on the platform. A large banner, NO CONSCRIPTION, is behind them. The hall is ringed with police. CLOSE-UP—Inspector Holliday, arms folded, standing at the back of the hall.)

(CLOSE-UP—Reitman, at the podium.)

REITMAN: As our last speaker of the evening, we had hoped to hear from Miss Emma Goldman. The authorities, however, have insisted that Miss Goldman be gagged.

(CUT TO—Emma, as she steps out from behind the stage with a handkerchief stuck in her mouth. The audience shrieks with laughter, stamps its feet, shouts its applause.)

REITMAN *(yelling above the din):*   So now we see that when you gag a voice, the voice becomes a roar!

(FREEZE.)

(CUT TO: Emma and Reitman, backstage.)

REITMAN: Perfect, my little blue-eyed mommy! What timing you have—a natural-born actress!

(Emma beams with pleasure. Reitman puts his arm around her, then signals to a photographer. A flash bulb goes off. Emma recoils.)

EMMA: No—no photographs!

(Reitman signals them to stop. He takes Emma in his arms.)

REITMAN: I want all the world to know what my mommy can do.

EMMA *(laughingly):*   Ben, for God's sakes—*you* can stay fifteen, but don't make me sixty!

(During the above exchange, Berkman is in the background, looking on disapprovingly.)

(Reitman and Emma kiss. FREEZE.)

(CUT TO: Berkman and Emma, in the apartment.)

BERKMAN: I tell you, it's absurd! The man's a clown!

EMMA: He says what he thinks and does what he wants.

BERKMAN: Indeed. But what he thinks is tripe and what he wants is publicity.

EMMA *(flaring):* The man stretches out his hand to us, and all you can see is that his fingernails are dirty!

BERKMAN: Emma, for God's sakes, face facts. Reitman knows nothing about our Cause, and cares less.

EMMA: He's worked tirelessly for us. We've never had such audiences. Yes, he's out of the ordinary. I thought that's what anarchists are sup-, posed to welcome in human nature?!

BERKMAN: There's no point in discussing it. You're infatuated with him.

EMMA: No. I'm in love with him.

BERKMAN: Don't be ridiculous. You couldn't possibly love such a creature. The man has no social sense.

EMMA *(blowing up):* You're a zealot, do you hear

me—a zealot! No one's ever good enough, perfect enough, pure enough! I'm sick of it, sick of it! Ever since your release, all I've heard is what's *wrong*: with me, with the movement, with Ben, with the world! I'm not an old woman. I want some *pleasure*. And Ben gives it to me. He loves me as a woman, not a symbol!

BERKMAN *(ice cold)*:   We will not discuss it again.

(FREEZE.)

(CUT TO: Emma, on platform. Ben next to her.)

EMMA: . . . While in San Francisco recently, I visited the Presidio, that beautiful spot overlooking the bay. Its purpose should have been playgrounds for children, gardens, and music for the weary. Instead it's full of ugly, gray barracks, where soldiers are herded like cattle, wasting their young days, drawn up in lines like convicts to salute every passing shrimp of a lieutenant. Along with being prisons, the barracks are centers for male prostitution.

(Gasps from the audience.)

EMMA: Does that surprise you? Then you haven't read your Havelock Ellis. In some regiments, the presumption is in *favor* of prostitution.

(A few catcalls.)

VOICE: Perversion!

EMMA: Are you cheering it up or down?

(More boos.)

VOICE: Are *you?*

EMMA: What I'm against is hypocrisy. I'm against convicting Oscar Wilde for acts that for him were natural and necessary. And practiced by half the aristocracy of England—the *male* half.

(Louder boos. Some tomatoes and eggs are thrown on the stage.)

EMMA *(calmly):*   Those of you who are friends: *Please*, don't respond. The police want nothing better than an excuse to call our meeting a riot and break it up.

(CLOSE-UP—Ben picking up some of the tomatoes and throwing them back at the audience.)

(CLOSE-UP—Emma, staring at him in disbelief.)

EMMA: Ben—for God's sakes!

(He retreats to his seat, grinning.)

EMMA *(to audience):*   Don't give the police a chance. Walk out quietly and you will help our cause a thousand times more than by answering the provocateurs. And as we walk out, let us sing.

(The audience applauds. Emma begins singing "The Internationale." It's picked up by the audience as it starts to file out.)

(CUT TO: Ben, as he leaps off the stage. He grabs the arm of an attractive young girl and marches out with her through the crowd.)

(CUT TO: Emma, scowling, hurt.)

(CUT TO: Emma in hotel room. Ben enters.)

EMMA: Ben, where have you *been*?

BEN: Looking for outlets for *Mother Earth.*

EMMA: For two days?!

BEN: Our contacts here are few. What's all the fuss?

EMMA: The "fuss" is that a major strike has broken out in the Lawrence textile mills. Bill Haywood's been calling since yesterday imploring me to come. One young girl's been shot and a young man bayoneted to death by a soldier. That's the "fuss"!

BEN: You should have gone.

EMMA: *You've* got the lecture receipts! Railroad tickets cost money.

BEN: Yes . . . well, we'll find it, that's all, we'll . . . find it.

EMMA: *Find* it? We've collected hundreds of dollars on the tour!

BEN: Emma, dearest, sit down for a minute.

EMMA *(pacing more agitatedly)*:   Tell it to me straight out. *Now.*

BEN: It's because of my mother, dearest. She depends on me as her sole support.

(CLOSE-UP—Emma's face: set, hard.)

EMMA: You've sent her some of the receipts.

BEN: I've always had to look after her. She has no one else.

EMMA: Who else have you been looking after?

BEN *(startled)*: You know I've worked day and night for the success of the tour. All I've asked is to be near you. Nothing else matters to me. Every day my passion for you grows.

EMMA: Your passion seems too large for one woman to contain.

BEN: Emma, dearest, you know you're the only person I care for, that without you I'd be—

EMMA *(interrupting furious)*: —Oh stop it, Ben! Stop all the lies! Let's have it out and get it over with! You've had women in every city we've been in. *That's* the truth of it!

BEN: Dearest, someone's been telling you—

EMMA: —the truth, Ben, the truth!

(His manner changes. His voice is quiet.)

BEN: They've never meant anything to me. Often I didn't know their names. But the physical attraction, I . . . it's like an obsession . . . something I can't control. . . . Don't send me away, Emma, I beg you. You're the only force in my life that matters. I'll prove myself if you only give me the chance. . . .

EMMA *(almost to herself)*:   Ah, Sasha, how well you knew. . . .

BEN: Sasha is *your* obsession. Sasha's always stood between us. I've never had a chance. Always I've been measured against Sasha! Sasha's suffering, Sasha's imprisonment, Sasha's sacrifice, Sasha's—

EMMA *(interrupting; cold fury)*:   —Sasha is not an obsession. Sasha is a *fact*. Would that I could say as much for you.

(As Emma moves to leave, DISSOLVE TO: Emma, Berkman, and Alice, in their New York apartment.)

EMMA: Perhaps I'm not fair. He comes from a world where lying is a way of life. What right have I to condemn him?

ALICE: But he himself says he didn't even love the women. You can't respect that.

EMMA: I'm not sure. Perhaps he's freer than we, despite all our talk. He acts on his needs, his lusts. Are they really so different from those we all have?

(Alice goes over and puts her arm around Emma.)

ALICE: You must try to forget him. He'll never bring you anything but pain.

(Emma looks over at Berkman, who sits impassively.)

EMMA: So, my twin? What do you say?

BERKMAN: Only you can say.

(FREEZE.)

(CUT TO: Emma, lying sleepless in her bed. She gets up, puts on her coat, and goes into the next room where Berkman and Alice are asleep in bed. She gently shakes Berkman awake.)

EMMA: I must go back to Ben. Will you take me?

(Without a word, Berkman gets up and starts to dress. She goes over and embraces him. He silently strokes her hair.)

(CLOSE-UP—Emma's face, her eyes full of tears.)

(CUT TO: Ben and Emma in a hotel room.)

BEN: It's too dangerous, Emma. I'd never forgive myself if anything happened to you. You can hear the crowd outside the hotel.

EMMA: All the more reason to give the lecture as announced.

(A knock at the door)

EMMA: Come in.

MESSENGER: You're wanted downstairs by the city authorities, Miss Goldman.

BEN: No, Emma, it's too dangerous. *(to messenger)* Tell the authorities that if they want to see Miss Goldman, they must come up here.

EMMA: Ben, we're in the biggest hotel in San

Diego. You're being timid.

(She starts after the messenger. Ben scurries after her.)

(DISSOLVE TO: Room, with six or seven men. One of them is the chief of police.)

CHIEF: This way, Miss Goldman, the mayor's waiting for you in the next room.

(Ben moves as if to follow her.)

CHIEF: Not you, Reitman. You wait here.

(CLOSE-UP—Emma entering the mayor's office. He immediately jumps up. Several others are in the room. Door closes behind Emma.)

(EXTERIOR—of mayor's office. CLOSE-UP—men grabbing Reitman, pinning his arms behind his back and thrusting a gag in his mouth. CLOSE-UP—Chief of police walks casually out of mayor's office. He walks past the men as if he hasn't seen a thing. The men hustle Reitman out of the room.)

(CUT TO: INTERIOR—mayor's office.)

MAYOR: The vigilantes are in an ugly mood, Miss Goldman. I feel it is my duty to warn you that if you persist in giving your speech tonight, anything could happen. A mob is forming outside the hotel.

EMMA: Then why don't you order it dispersed? There's an ordinance, I believe, against obstructing traffic in the business district.

MAYOR: We're prepared to offer you safe passage out of town if you agree to leave now.

EMMA *(sardonic):*   That's very kind of you.

MAYOR: I warn you. It's a patriotic crowd.

EMMA: I've never accepted protection from the police, and I don't intend to now. I charge all of you in this room with direct complicity with the vigilantes.

(She wheels around to leave.)

MAYOR *(calling after her):*   You'll have only your- self to blame!

EMMA: How profoundly I wish that were true.

(CUT TO: The outer office, as Emma enters. CLOSE- UP—Her face, shocked, as she scans the empty space. She rushes into the hotel lobby. CLOSE-UP— Chief of police, leaning casually against the side.)

EMMA: Where's Reitman? What have you done with him?

CHIEF: Reitman? Reitman? Oh yeah—that guy they call the king of the hobos. My guess would be he's out in the country, trampin' it.

EMMA: If any harm comes to him, you'll pay for it, you hear? Even if I have to use my own hands.

(The chief guffaws.)

(CUT TO: Emma's hotel room. Emma is pacing frantically. The phone rings.)

EMMA: Yes?

VOICE: Reitman will be aboard the 2:45 A.M. train for Los Angeles. If you're not on it, Reitman will never be seen again.

EMMA: Is he alive? Who is this? Is he alive?

(Click at the other end.)

(CUT TO: Emma, standing by the boarding platform of the train. She looks nervously to all sides. No one else is in sight. As if from nowhere, a man suddenly steps to her side.)

MAN: Reitman is in the rear car. Bon voyage to you both.

(He tips his hat and holds out a small American flag. Emma rushes inside the train.)

(CUT TO: Emma, running through the railroad car. She catches sight of Ben's form huddled up in the rear seat. He's in blue overalls, his face deathly pale, his hair sticky with tar, his eyes open but terrified.)

(CUT TO: Emma, cradling him in her arms.)

EMMA: Oh, my boy, my poor boy . . .

REITMAN: Mommy, oh, Mommy . . . am I alive? . . . am I alive?

EMMA: S-sh. Yes dearest, Mommy is here, it's all right now . . . Mommy is here.

REITMAN *(crying):*   . . . beat me everywhere . . .

said they'd kill me . . . twisted testicles . . .
cane up my rectum . . .

(Between Reitman's broken phrases, Emma tries to comfort and shush him.)

REITMAN: Mommy . . . look.

(He opens his shirt. ZOOM to his chest: The letters "U.S.A." have been branded there.)

(FREEZE.)

(CUT TO: Ben, limping around the living room of a new apartment, carrying a book. Emma's at work writing.)

BEN *(grumpily)*:   Mama wants more tea.

EMMA: Ben, can't you, for heaven's sakes, boil some water?! Or can't *she*?

BEN: You could at least *try* to be nice to her. It's difficult for an old woman to pull up roots and come live in a strange city.

EMMA: That's what *I* said when you broached the idea. The poor thing's lost without her pots and kettles.

(The apartment doorbell rings.)

EMMA: It's Sasha. And I still haven't finished the article.

BEN: Don't bother with the tea.

EMMA: I had no intention of bothering.

(Ben exits. Emma goes to the door. She and Berkman embrace.)

EMMA: I'm sorry, dearest. I don't have the lead ready. Mrs. Reitman has been the center of all attention.

BERKMAN: I've brought good news. The Post Office has agreed to release the January issue.

EMMA: Marvelous!

BERKMAN: The chief inspector has dismissed Comstock's complaint as groundless. Comstock now claims that *Mother Earth* was held up not as a result of a complaint by him, but as a deliberate scheme of *yours* to attract publicity.

EMMA: Only Anthony Comstock could simultaneously object to an article on prostitution and then publicly prostitute himself.

(They laugh.)

BERKMAN: Frankly, I think Woodrow Wilson is going to cause us more trouble than Anthony Comstock. Now that the conscription bill is law, the patriots are going to be in full cry.

(Ben throws open the door.)

BEN *(majestically)*:   Emma—we've had the most glorious idea!

BERKMAN *(hurriedly, to Emma, as he slips out the door)*:   Bring the piece to the office. I'll hold up the printing.

(As Ben strides into the center of the room, the figure of his mother appears behind him, framed in the doorway.)

BEN: We're going to start a Sunday school class! Right *here.*

MOTHER: Jesus in the sanctum of the atheist.

BEN: It's my calling. I know it now. It's the only way to bring the message of peace. The voice of the Nazarene speaking directly to the young.

EMMA *(wearily)*:   Oh Ben, do what you want. *(turns back to her desk)*

BEN: That's all you have to say to me?

EMMA: You are *not* the Nazarene. Though your mother apparently believes otherwise. And so might the young women who will doubtless flock to your classes.

BEN: No, not to you! To you I'm an office boy. Someone to arrange your tours, carry your luggage, peddle your little magazine, get beaten up by—

(Emma explodes. She picks up a chair and hurls it at Ben.)

EMMA: I've had enough! Enough of you and your mother! Get her out of here! Today! *Now!* And get yourself out too!

(FREEZE.)

(CUT TO: The office of Mother Earth. *Emma, Berkman, Alice, and several friends are all busy with the magazine—typing, preparing layouts, etc. Suddenly there's the sound of heavy stamping of feet on the stairway. A dozen men burst into the office, led by a federal marshal.)*

MARSHAL: Emma Goldman! Alexander Berkman! You're under arrest.

EMMA: And who are you?

MARSHAL: United States Marshal Thomas D. McCarthy.

EMMA: I would like to see your warrant.

(McCarthy holds out a copy of Mother Earth.*)*

MARSHAL: Are you the author of the No-Conscription article published in this magazine?

EMMA: Obviously, since my name is signed to it. I take full responsibility for everything in the magazine! Now where is your warrant.

MARSHAL: I represent the United States government.

(He signals his men to seize Emma and Berkman. Others start ransacking the desks and overturning the press.)

MARSHAL: Get everything: subscription lists, files, manuscripts—everything.

EMMA: You'll find the most treasonable matter, Mr. McCarthy—*(pointing to books on shelves)*—on those shelves. The volumes by Tolstoy, Thoreau, and George Bernard Shaw.

MARSHAL: Are they employees of your press?

EMMA *(laughing)*:   Inspirers, perhaps. Not employees.

MARSHAL *(to policemen)*:   Seize those books!

EMMA: I do hope you'll put us all on trial together. I've always wanted to meet Mr. Shaw.

(FREEZE.)

(CUT TO: Courtroom. Emma and Berkman stand before the U.S. Commissioner.

COMMISSIONER: The grand jury has brought in an indictment charging you with conspiracy to defeat the draft. Bail is set at twenty-five thousand dollars each.

BERKMAN: Twenty-five thousand? The same sum the newspapers say the Kaiser has paid us. What a pity he's been so tardy in forwarding the money.

(A man steps forward.)

MAN: As representative of the friends of the two defendants, I am empowered to offer as their bond, real estate certificates to the value of three hundred thousand dollars.

COMMISSIONER: Refused. Only cash is acceptable.

(to Emma and Berkman) You are to be re-manded to the Tombs. Trial to be in five days, on June 27.

EMMA: My forty-eighth birthday, Mr. Commissioner. I could not wish for a more appropriate celebration.

(FREEZE.)

(CUT TO: Courtroom. Judge Mayer presiding. Emma and Berkman stand before the bench.)

BERKMAN: As it is the evident intention of the government to turn this prosecution into persecution, we have decided to take no part in the proceedings.

JUDGE MAYER: The court will appoint counsel to defend you.

BERKMAN: We want no counsel.

JUDGE MAYER: In our country even the poorest are accorded the benefit of legal defense.

EMMA: We are not the poorest.

BERKMAN: We have each written a brief statement which we wish to deliver. Beyond that, we are indifferent. We do not believe in the possibility of justice from these proceedings.

(JUMP CUT TO: The trial. "The Star-Spangled Banner" is being played. Most of the courtroom is standing at attention. Emma and Berkman remain seated.)

(CUT TO: Front row, where Alice and several other friends also remain seated. They are removed forcibly by the guards.)

(CUT TO: Berkman, finishing the reading of his statement to the court.)

BERKMAN: . . . This hearing is purely an inquiry into my views. I deny the right of anyone to set up an inquisition of thought. For the government to attempt to prescribe certain opinions is the height of despotism. This hearing is an invasion of my conscience. I therefore refuse, most emphatically, to participate in it.

(He sits down.)

JUDGE MAYER: Miss Goldman.

(She rises. Unlike Berkman, she has no notes and speaks extemporaneously.)

EMMA: The United States government is engaged in the farce of undertaking to carry democracy abroad by suppressing the last vestiges of it at home. The judge has admonished the jury that in this country "only such ideas are permissible as are 'within the law.'" There has never been a humane ideal which in its time has been considered "within the law." I name Jesus, Socrates, Galileo, Giordano Bruno. I name, too, those great Americans Thomas Jefferson and Patrick Henry who broke the law in order to set America free from British rule. I name other great Americans—William Lloyd Garrison, John Brown, Wendell Phillips—who broke the law in order to challenge the crime of human slavery

193 • • •

which the law then upheld. . . . The real and terrible menace of these proceedings is that they are designed to exile those who do not fit into the scheme of things our industrial lords are so eager to perpetuate. . . . With all the power and intensity of my being, I protest against the conspiracy of imperialist capitalism against the life and the liberty of the American people.

(FREEZE.)

(JUMP CUT TO: Judge Mayer pronouncing sentence.)

JUDGE MAYER: The jury has found you guilty.

(Emma jumps to her feet.)

EMMA: I move the verdict be set aside as absolutely contrary to the evidence.

JUDGE MAYER: Motion denied.

EMMA: I further move that sentencing be deferred for at least several days so we may have the chance of consultation.

JUDGE MAYER: Denied. Do the defendants have anything to say as to why sentence should not be imposed?

BERKMAN: We have been convicted because we are anarchists, because we have a dream of universal brotherhood. I defy you to show us where we have once told a lie.

JUDGE MAYER: We have no place in our country for

those who would nullify our laws. I shall recommend to the immigration authorities that you be deported from the country—at once. The court is adjourned.

(The judge turns to leave the bench. CLOSE-UP— Emma's defiant face.)

EMMA: One moment, please. Are we to be denied even a few days to gather up our things?

JUDGE MAYER: The prisoners are remanded to the custody of the United States Marshal.

(The judge again turns to leave.)

EMMA: One more word please! *(bows low)* I want to thank Your Honor for his kindness in refusing us a stay of even two days, a stay you would have accorded the most heinous criminal. I thank you, sir, for your remarkable humanity.

(CLOSE-UP—Judge Mayer's face, white and angry. He moves his lips as if to speak, then abruptly turns and leaves the bench.)

(FREEZE.)

(CUT TO: The Buford. We're at the moment just prior to scene one, act one. Berkman and Alice are embracing at the gangplank. A few friends are hugging Emma and pressing flowers on her.)

(CLOSE-UP—Berkman and Alice.)

ALICE: Somehow, dear . . . I'll join you somehow. . . .

(Berkman hugs her silently.)

(MONTAGE: Earlier gangplank sequence with re-porters from scene one, act one. The only lines heard are the final two:)

REPORTER: This is the end, Emma Goldman, isn't it?

EMMA: No. Only another beginning.

(Emma's voice is heard over scenes of debarka-tion.)

EMMA *(voice-over):*   January 20, 1920. Dearest Alice: I write to you on what is apparently our last night on the *Buford*. We have finally been told that we are to be landed at Hango, a Finnish port, given three days' rations, and from there speeded in locked trains to the Russian border. So after all these years, it is again to be *Ma-tushka Rossiya*. Once more home; once more an immigrant without a home. You know how I welcomed the revolution, how I bless the hope it may be *the* revolution we have all worked for so long. Yet already it is a state—even though a Bolshevist one—and you know my fears of *any* state. Sasha doesn't share my doubts. I wonder. Can *any* state fail to become oppressive? Is it not in the nature of governing, of ruling others? Sometimes I fear Russia may not be so good as America. How I already long for the land that has made me suffer so! Have I not also known love and joy there? . . . They say I was not a patriot. They aren't used to patriots who love rather than worship, who are under the beloved's spell but not blind to the beloved's defects. I cannot forget America. But now after all these years I'm to behold again *Matushka Rossiya*, and my heart starts to beat for that. Sasha says we will behold her freed at last from her ancient political and economic masters—the *dubinushka* raised from the dust, the worker in a world of his own creating. Ah, how I hope, my Alice, how I hope. . . . Perhaps a dream is to begin . . . perhaps a nightmare . . .

(CUT TO: Emma, Berkman, and Bill Haywood in an apartment in Petrograd.)

EMMA: The receptions, Bill, we've been over-whelmed with receptions! How good to be with an old friend—and an American one!

HAYWOOD: American? You're looking back!

BERKMAN: It's been inspiring beyond words. Who would have believed it, after centuries of repression: a spontaneous break for freedom by *the great masses themselves*. And to be welcomed as brothers, after being sent from America as felons!

EMMA: We expected you at the border. Didn't you get our radiogram? It seemed every three seconds soldiers were shining flashlights into our faces, demanding our pass cards. Oh, and some of the people along the road, Bill! So pale faced and sad! We've even heard of a secret police. It can't be, can it, Bill?—the people *made* the revolution, the people must be—

HAYWOOD *(interrupting)*:   —Emma, *Emma*! I see you haven't changed a bit. Still the same old persistent pest!

BERKMAN *(to Haywood)*:   Save your words. We've

already been through it a dozen times. Emma seems unable to grasp that revolution in practice is not the same as revolution in theory.

HAYWOOD: Emma, be patient. For once in your life, be patient. Russia is ringed with enemies. You have no idea of conditions: the allied blockade, the intervention, the counterrevolutionary plotters. You can't create a new world in a day.

EMMA But you can destroy one. I've even heard of jailing political prisoners, of denying free speech, of—

HAYWOOD (*interrupting, less affectionate*): —Emma, I'm going to be stern with you. You anarchists have always been the romantics of revolution. You've never understood the fearful cost it would entail, the fierce determination of its enemies to destroy it. You cannot fight fire and sword with an ideal.

EMMA: My dear Bill, you cannot fight it any other way—not, that is, without losing the ideal. (*to Berkman*) I thought that was the one lesson we'd learned—that means become ends.

BERKMAN (*furious*): I won't hear any more of this sentimentality! You've been on Russian soil a matter of days, and already, in your imperious way, you've mapped the continent! Our job is to make ourselves useful, not to throw up petty objections to every deviation from bourgeois principle! I won't hear any more of it—is that clear?!

HAYWOOD (*calmly*): Sasha's right, Emma. Find

useful work. Talk to the comrades. Meet our leaders. Lenin himself is aware of your arrival, and has expressed a willingness to meet you. Emma: The baby you've labored all your life to bring to birth *has* at last been born. Don't berate it for not yet speaking perfect sentences!

EMMA (*quietly*):   You must be right. So many good people are saying the same. . . . I must work. I must work hard. And wait . . .

(FREEZE.)

(CUT TO: Entrance to office of People's Commissar for Education. Berkman and Emma are repeatedly stopped by sentries and asked for their propusks *[pass cards], until finally they are let into the inner office of Commissar Lunacharsky.)*

(CUT TO: Inner office. The conversation is already in progress.)

LUNACHARSKY: . . . You can be an invaluable help, coming as you do from the United States. We are introducing the American system of education throughout Soviet Russia.

EMMA (*astonished*):   But that system is outmoded— rigid and authoritarian. Some of the finest pedagogical minds in America, like John Dewey, have put it under indictment. It should hardly serve as a model in revolutionary Russia!

LUNACHARSKY: You must understand the problem we labor under. Many of the children are defectives; centuries of mistreatment. Without discipline, illiteracy will never disappear.

(CLOSE-UP—Emma's dismayed look, and Berkman's uncomfortable one, as Lunacharsky goes on.)

LUNACHARSKY *(dismissive)*: But of course we must hear the new ideas, too. A conference, perhaps. A special conference. We will notify you.

(FREEZE on Emma's astonished face. When her face reanimates, she is talking with a Soviet doctor.)

DOCTOR: The task is colossal. The dearth of medical supplies, the wretched condition of the hospitals. It is almost overwhelming. . . .

EMMA: I'm a trained nurse. I'll do my utmost.

DOCTOR: I expect nothing less from a tovarich. I've been told of your great work in the Communist movement in America.

EMMA: The anarchist movement.

DOCTOR: Oh, yes. But there is really no difference.

EMMA: There is every difference. The coercion of state communism has no relationship to the voluntary cooperation of anarchistic communism. That, however, won't affect my usefulness as a nurse.

DOCTOR *(coldly)*: In Soviet Russia everyone who wants to work is welcome. So long as he is a true revolutionist.

EMMA: I will defend the revolution to my last

breath. But that is not the same as defending the dictatorship of the state.

DOCTOR: Your application will have to go through channels. It may take several months.

EMMA: But you said the need was urgent!

DOCTOR: We will contact you.

(FREEZE.)

(CUT TO: Berkman and Emma, in their room. Berkman is showing her a manuscript.)

BERKMAN: It is by Lenin. Radek has asked me to translate it.

EMMA: An important assignment, Sashenka. You must be pleased.

BERKMAN: I've refused.

EMMA: Why?

BERKMAN: It's an attack on anarchists as "infantile leftists," counterrevolutionaries. I told Radek I would translate it only if allowed to add a preface. Radek said, "Lenin's work is not prefaced."

(FREEZE.)

(CUT TO: Berkman and Emma, in the streets. They are stopped by armed members of the Cheka police and pushed to a wall. Their papers are examined. The leader of the police bows in apology to the "foreign tovarich" and moves on.

Berkman and Emma enter a small market area. Old woman, children in tatters, and derelict men immediately cluster around them, trying to sell their wares: ill-smelling soup, hard biscuits, a few boxes of matches. They hold out the wares with trembling hands. One old woman speaks in a shaky voice.)

WOMAN: Buy, *barinya*, oi Christo, buy!

(The Cheka police reappear. Immediately, the people flee. The Cheka pours out the soup in the square and breaks the matches. One or two of the older people are seized.)

(CLOSE-UP—Berkman, averting his face.)

(CUT TO: Emma, in the office of Zinoviev, head of the Third International.)

EMMA: . . . But the Bolsheviki have always stressed the potency of hunger.

ZINOVIEV: Hunger is due to the Allied blockade.

EMMA: But dear comrade, must the city freeze, too? Petrograd is surrounded by woodland.

ZINOVIEV: The blockade has destroyed transportation.

EMMA: But if the people were allowed, they could simply go out with pick and ax and ropes and haul home enough wood for their own use. There is so much misery from the cold.

ZINOVIEV: It would interfere with revolutionary discipline.

EMMA: The population has been reduced from a million and a half to four hundred thousand.

ZINOVIEV: Thanks to the blockade. And the enemies within. Power must be centralized in the party, or there is no chance to combat the revolution's enemies.

(FREEZE.)

(CUT TO: Berkman and Emma, in their room.)

EMMA: It's worse than the Okhrana! Persecution, suffering everywhere. Bureaucracy, centralization! The Revolution's been betrayed, Sasha! Why won't you see it?!

BERKMAN: Your standard is the fate of individuals. You can't measure a gigantic upheaval by a few specks of dust.

EMMA: Abstract rubbish! When individual lives don't matter, revolutionary ethics have been betrayed.

BERKMAN: Revolution in a primitive country with an ignorant populace cannot survive without drastic measures.

EMMA: *Against* the people?

BERKMAN: You exaggerate. As always. You have to distinguish between the Revolution and the regime. I agree they are currently worlds apart, and the abyss may grow wider still. But the Revolution itself must be protected. We cannot give fuel to its enemies by denouncing the regime.

EMMA: But the regime is killing the Revolution. If there's *any* chance of saving it, we must denounce the men who have captured and misdirected it. *(suddenly stops, struck with an idea)* Balabanoff. We'll go to see Angelica Balabanoff. She will tell us the truth.

(FREEZE.)

(CUT TO: Berkman and Emma in Balabanoff's small room. The latter, a middle-aged woman with large sad eyes, lies ill on a couch. In front of her is a samovar, some fruit jelly, biscuits, and butter, which she is having difficulty serving. Emma rises to help her.)

EMMA: Please, Miss Balabanoff, let me help.

BALABANOFF: You must call me Angelica. I'm sorry to be unwell for your visit. Why did you wait so long before coming? You should have let me know at once.

BERKMAN: We knew how busy you are.

BALABANOFF: Was. Now that I'm no longer secretary of the International, there is much time.

EMMA: The rumor is that your opposition to party centralization led to your deposition.

BALABANOFF: Even a rumor has occasionally been known to be true.

EMMA: Then you agree with me, Angelica! Bureaucratic poison is killing the Revolution!

BALABANOFF: Eat something, dear. Alexander? I

feel so guilty enjoying these luxuries, when people have no bread. Friends bring them. So maybe it is not so sinful.

(Emma starts to weep.)

BALABANOFF: My dearest Emma, what have I said?! Are you ill, dear? What did I do?

(Emma embraces her, stroking her thick braided hair.)

EMMA: No, no . . . it's just that . . . you're kind, Angelica. We've had so many shocks . . . it's all been such a . . . nightmare.

BERKMAN: Is it true that many anarchists are in prison?

BALABANOFF: Yes.

EMMA: Isn't there any way to put a stop to such things?

BALABANOFF: Not within Russia. The Cheka. And no one would think of a protest abroad so long as the Revolution is in danger.

EMMA: I would think of it. Because the Revolution's chief enemy is Lenin, his party and his state.

BALABANOFF: Perhaps the chief enemy is life itself—the rock that breaks the finest spirits, the best intentions.

EMMA *(agitated)*: Life! Life! But what is life but

the genius people impart to it? And what is the use of striving if some mysterious power called life can turn it all to naught?

(Pause.)

BALABANOFF: You must see Lenin. He knows how to meet life's demands in full measure.

BERKMAN: You and Lenin are still in contact?

BALABANOFF: I'm a helpless—and friendly—woman. I'll arrange the interview for you.

(FREEZE.)

(CUT TO: An armed guard. He waves Emma and Berkman ahead, he unlocks an elevator, motions them into it, locks it behind them, and puts the key in his pocket. On the first floor a soldier shouts the names "Goldman and Berkman." The shouted names are repeated on the second, third, etc. floors. At the top floor, the guard repeats the process of unlocking and locking the elevator.)

(They are then ushered into a vast, empty reception hall, as yet another guard shouts "Tovarichy Goldman and Berkman." A young man appears from nowhere and leads them silently to a massive, ornately carved door. It opens from within.)

(CLOSE-UP—Lenin, behind a huge desk, his piercing eyes fixed directly on Emma and Berkman as they enter. Everything on the desk and in the room is arranged with absolute precision. Lenin brandishes a brochure in his hand.)

LENIN: Ah, Comrades Goldman and Berkman.

Angelica has sent me the transcript of your trial and speeches. You used your opportunity splendidly. It is worth going to prison, if the courts can be successfully turned into a forum.

EMMA AND BERKMAN: Thank you.

LENIN: And when can we expect the social revolution in America?

(CLOSE-UP—Emma's astonished face.)

LENIN: In the near future? What of the labor movement? Is it honeycombed with bourgeois ideology, or is that only true of Gompers and his clique? What of the rank and file? Are they fertile soil for boring from within?

BERKMAN: At the moment, the situation in America does not look promising for social revolution. Less promising than, say, twenty years ago. The war has destroyed much of the radical movement, coopting and fragmenting it. And in many cases, like our own, the government has resorted to outright repression and deportation.

(Lenin again brandishes the brochure.)

LENIN: A pity you couldn't have remained in America. Fighters are badly needed there.

EMMA: The choice was not ours. We were deported.

LENIN: You are most welcome in Soviet Russia. You, Berkman, what an organizer you must be; true metal! Many anarchists hold important positions with us. Everything is open to them if they are willing to cooperate with us.

EMMA: I am proud to hear my anarchist comrades praised so highly, tovarich Lenin. But why then are so many in Soviet prisons? We have seen them ourselves.

LENIN: Nonsense! How could you believe such propaganda against the Revolution?! We have *bandits* in prison—the followers of Makhno— only bandits.

EMMA: But we have learned that anarchists may not speak their minds—without risk of imprisonment.

LENIN: Free speech is a *bourgeois* diversion. In the Workers' Republic economic well-being talks louder than speech, and its freedom is far more secure. The Revolution is under attack on all sides from its enemies. To prattle of free speech is to give those enemies ammunition. Only bandits are guilty of that; which is why they are under lock and key. . . . What work do you want to do for the Revolution?

BERKMAN: The Moscow Anarchist Conference—

EMMA *(interrupting):*   —which had to meet in secret—

BERKMAN: —has asked us to present these resolutions to you. They emphasize that our comrades in jail are not bandits. They call on the Soviets to legalize anarchism.

LENIN *(taking the document; perfunctorily):*   I will

bring it up at the next session of the Party Executive. *(sternly)* These trifles, however, must not be allowed to absorb revolutionary energies. Now: What work do you want to do for the Revolution?

EMMA: In America, tovarich, we fought for the political rights even of our opponents. The denial of them here to our comrades is therefore no trifle to us. I, for one, cannot cooperate with a regime that persecutes opinion.

LENIN: You don't seem to understand, tovarich Goldman, that we are engaged in a life-and-death struggle. Small considerations cannot be permitted to weigh in the struggle. Russia has ignited a world revolution. *Do* something to help it. That will be the best way of regaining your revolutionary balance.

BERKMAN: We have given some thought to organizing a society called Russian Friends of American Freedom, a body to give active support to America's struggle for liberty.

(Lenin gives a hearty belly laugh.)

LENIN: A brilliant idea! Splendid, splendid! You shall have all the help you need—an office, printers, couriers, funds—everything you need. You must start at once. Send me immediately your prospectus of work, and I will introduce it under the auspices of the Third International. That is the proper channel for the venture.

(CLOSE-UP—Emma and Berkman, exchanging an apprehensive look.)

BERKMAN: We feel our efforts would be most effective if free from any affiliation with known Bolshevik organizations.

EMMA: We can best carry out the work in our own way. We know the American psychology and how best to approach it.

(The young man who guided them into the office suddenly reappears and motions them to the door.)

LENIN: Send me the prospectus. Do not delay.

(FREEZE.)

(CUT TO: Berkman and Emma in their room; he is writing, Emma reading. The faint noises of cannonading are suddenly heard. At the sound of the firing, Berkman is frozen. Emma jumps up in horror.)

EMMA: Oh no! Oh, Sasha, my God—they've done it! They've started to bombard Kronstadt!

BERKMAN *(quietly)*:   I didn't believe they'd do it. I didn't believe it. The Soviet government in arms against its own dissenters. The last thread is broken.

(They hold to each other; Emma starts to cry.)

EMMA: It's as if you wanted a child all your life, and at last, when you had almost given up hoping, it had been given to you—only to die soon after its birth.

BERKMAN: If there was something we could do . . .

EMMA: We must leave Russia, Sashenka. It's all death here, blood and betrayal. And no hope of being heard. Perhaps at least we can warn the rest of the world.

BERKMAN: I'm ready to go, dear. I'm ready.

(FREEZE.)

(MONTAGE under the voice-over below.)

(Emma and Berkman packing.)

(Tearfully embracing Balabanoff and others.)

(Sitting on a train, their faces tear-streaked, their arms entwined.)

EMMA *(voice-over):*   O radiant dream, O burning faith! O dream of Revolutionary rebirth, of life purged of hate and strife, of liberated humanity, embracing all. Gone, all gone, the dream crushed, the faith broken, my heart like stone.

(CUT TO: Emma, on platform.)

EMMA: . . . This is what we have come to England to tell you. The dream is become a nightmare. The Revolution is become a dictatorship, as bad as any in the days of the czar. Terror has silenced the masses and the intellectuals alike. Those few who have spoken out have been shot in the cellars of the Cheka. Lev Tchorny's old mother called daily at the prison, pleading for his life. The Cheka assured her he would not be executed. And indeed they kept their promise. They didn't have to kill Tchorny outright. He obliged them by dying gradually from the inflicted torture. . . . Our beloved Fanya Baron is another. Our dear, splendid Fanya, radiant with life and love.

(CLOSE-UP—Emma, trying to hold back the tears.)

EMMA: *Existy*, they called her, "expropriator." She fought to her last breath. They had to drag her, then carry her to the Cheka cellar, where the knights of the Communist state shot her through the head. *(starts to cry.)* I make no apology for my tears. They're shed for some of the loveliest spirits the world has ever known.

(FREEZE)

(CUT TO: Emma and Berkman on reception line. As each person approaches Emma, his or her name is announced.)

VOICE: Dr. Havelock Ellis.

ELLIS *(to Emma, as he shakes her hand):*   My own feeling is that Russia must work out things in her own way. Every social condition is, in some degree, affected by the social condition that preceded it. And if that was cruel, what follows cannot be entirely good.

(FOCUS BLURS.)

VOICE: Mr. Bertrand Russell.

RUSSELL: I am persuaded, Miss Goldman, that the cruelties would be at least as great under any other party. And I do not regard the abolition of all government as a thing which has any chance of being brought forth in our lifetime. . . . I am therefore unwilling to be associated with any movement which might seem to imply that a change of government is desirable in Russia.

EMMA: You never hesitated to use your pen, Mr. Russell, in behalf of the political victims of the czar. Should we now sit supinely by while the Soviet state commits murder?

(The announcing voice becomes increasingly "surreal," echoey. "Professor Harold Laski . . . Mr. H. G. Wells . . ." At the same time, camera gradually blurs from the reception line to a MONTAGE of Emma and Berkman moving from hotel to hotel, from country to country. The voice-overs become increasingly shrill and denunciatory:

VOICE *(voice-overs):* By speaking and writing publicly against the Bolshevik government, you, Emma Goldman, have betrayed the international proletariat and given invaluable ammunition to reactionary forces everywhere . . .

What you apparently don't realize, Miss Goldman, is that the Bolsheviks are in the saddle in Russia because they have the confidence of all Russia . . .

Your emphasis on Russia's sins is out of all proportion to her gains. Perhaps it's because you and Berkman weren't treated as celebrities. If you had been less egotistical, you would have offered your labor to the Workers' Republic, cheerfully doing whatever needed doing instead of spending your energy on complaint and recrimination . . .

Out of respect for our past friendship, I think it's better if we never see each other again. I don't want to have to think of you with bitterness . . .

(MONTAGE continues. Emma and Berkman packing and unpacking. Date cards denote the passage of years: 1921, 1923, 1925, 1928, 1930. Also VISUALS to suggest a variety of countries: England, Germany, Sweden, Canada. The sense of exile, of eternal wandering, of no place to lay their heads.)

(CUT TO: Small cottage in Saint-Tropez. Emma and Berkman are going over a manuscript.)

BERKMAN: I'd change the line to read this way: "Slavery is slavery. I care not whether it be called a collective society or a capitalist one. The only difference is in a change of masters."

EMMA: Yes, Sasha, that's much better. You're the writer. I'd never be able to complete this without you.

(Berkman motions to the huge pile of manuscript.)

BERKMAN: I'd like to cut still more of it. A thousand pages! Emma, it's unwieldy!

EMMA: My life's been that way. So should the book about it. No, old pal, no more cuts.

BERKMAN *(good-naturedly)*:   One or two of the love affairs could go.

EMMA: Nonsense! I hope to add one or two more before the book's in proofs. I'm only sixty-one, old pal! Now take that young fisherman who's been giving me the eye . . .

BERKMAN: He's after your money.

(They laugh.)

EMMA: He probably does think we're millionaires, living here in posh Saint-Tropez. You're quite right, I'll have to scrutinize his motives carefully. Though hopefully he'll prevent that by talking to me only in French.

BERKMAN: I think you should call the book *Living My Life*. You're one of the few who's done it, old girl.

EMMA: Don't use the past tense! There's much ahead.

BERKMAN: Emma, my love, we're two homeless old people living in a cottage, with a few loyal friends paying the rent.

EMMA: And what of the letter just today asking us to join the international defense committee for Sacco and Vanzetti?

BERKMAN *(sadly)*:   Emma, Emma . . . Dearest, there's no place left for us to gain a footing, no chance to throw in our lot with those who continue the struggle.

EMMA: Chances are made. With fascism spreading all over Europe, two toothless tigers can do a lot of growling. We might go on the vaudeville circuit; I hear they pay two thousand a week.

BERKMAN: To clowns.

EMMA: Perfect! We haven't laughed enough lately.

(They laugh. Pause.)

BERKMAN: I wish the book wasn't nearly finished.

It filled up a lot of time. Life has become a stupid thing.

EMMA (*seriously*):   Alexander Berkman, I've seen all sides of you. But one side I've never seen—and don't believe exists—is self-pity. We're very far from retirement. Our lives are going to end as they began: fighting.

(*He goes over and kisses her.*)

BERKMAN: Yours, dear Emma, without doubt. I seem to have forgotten the habit.

(*CLOSE-UP—Emma's concerned look. She strokes Berkman's head gently.*)

EMMA (*softly*):   We might even tour America again. John Dewey, Dreiser, Mencken—all kinds of wonderful people are working for our return.

BERKMAN: It's you they want, old girl . . . you . . .

EMMA (*almost to herself*):   Why does that country keep its grip on my heart? No matter where else we go, I feel an alien. It's disgraceful in a revolutionist to feel so rooted in the soil of one place. Why, Sasha, why?

BERKMAN: Because the place is like you, Emma: always believing in possibilities.

(*As they sit silently on the couch, DISSOLVE TO: Emma, asleep in her bed. She's awakened suddenly by the loud sound of gunshot. She jumps out of bed and rushes into the next room. Berkman is lying in a pool of blood on the living room floor. She rushes up to him and takes him in her arms.*)

EMMA *(distraught)*:   Sasha . . . Sashenka . . . oh no . . . oh, no, dearest . . .

BERKMAN *(grim smile)*:   I think I've bungled it, old girl . . . bungled it again. . . . I guess Johann Most was right: These Russians can't shoot straight.

EMMA: Why have you done such a thing? . . . Why? . . . Why? . . . *(she cradles him in her arms)*

BERKMAN: It's time I cleared out, old girl. . . . I can't live useless . . . dependent . . . you still have much to give . . . go on, dear old girl . . . go on . . .

(He dies. As Emma sobs convulsively over his body, FREEZE.)

(CUT TO: Emma, on the beach at Saint-Tropez. She's walking slowly near the water's edge, dressed in winter clothes. At first she seems to be alone. But then, behind her, the CAMERA PICKS UP the figure of Helena, bent down by the water's edge, examining shells.)

HELENA: Emma—come see!

(CLOSE-UP—Helena's hand, holding a shell.)

HELENA: Have you ever seen so deep a purple?! Like on the Kexholm, near St. Petersburg.

EMMA: It's lovely, isn't it.

(CAMERA PANS away from the two women down

the beach, deserted except for the figure of a man moving toward them. The man [Augustine Souchy] starts to run. Emma and Helena see him coming and exchange an anxious look. He comes up to them, out of breath.)

SOUCHY: Miss Goldman? Is one of you Miss Goldman?

EMMA: Yes, I am.

SOUCHY: Oh, thank heavens! I was so afraid you'd have left Saint-Tropez. The people in town said they haven't seen you in weeks.

EMMA: This is my sister, Helena.

(He bows.)

SOUCHY: Yes, of course. Excuse me. I mean, frightening you this way. But I was told to deliver the message personally, and I was so afraid that you'd already gone.

EMMA: Catch your breath.

SOUCHY: Thank you, yes. *(breathes deeply)* Allow me to introduce myself. I am Augustine Souchy, secretary of the Comité Anarcho-Syndicaliste.

EMMA *(startled)*:   From Barcelona?!

SOUCHY: The same.

EMMA *(embracing him)*:   My dear Souchy, what an honor! But I . . . I'm astonished . . . !

SOUCHY: I come bearing an invitation. From the

Confederación Nacional del Trabajo. *And* the Federación Anarquista Ibérica. *(hands her a letter)* An official invitation.

EMMA *(near tears)*:   My dear Souchy—what in God's name does it say?! I can't be reading letters! I can barely keep my hands steady!

SOUCHY *(reading)*:   "The military chiefs under Franco have determined to crush the anarchist communes. In Catalonia we are just as determined to resist. The people have thrown up barricades everywhere. The comrades ask you to come. Ten thousand workers in Barcelona wait to greet you. Durruti himself begged me to say to you: Emma Goldman, you must come. The ideal you have fought for everywhere is here in Catalonia alive—a people without rulers, living in harmony. Come to us. We need your strength."

(Emma, in tears, embraces him. CAMERA PANS away as the three figures hurry off down the beach.)

VOICE *(voice-over)*:   Emma Goldman gave the last years of her life to the fight in Spain against Franco. She died in 1940 of a stroke. The United States Immigration and Naturalization Service granted the dead exile reentry into the country, where she was buried in Chicago's Waldheim Cemetery, near the graves of her Haymarket comrades.

(As voice-over continues, rerun of scene one, act one: Emma on the rail of the Buford *as it moves out to sea. The Statue of Liberty appears in the background.)*

VOICE *(voice-over):* One day in Spain Emma was taken high into the Pyrenees to see an anarchist experiment in education. She was greeted by a large banner which spelled out in bold letters the name of the colony: MON NOU: NEW WORLD. Under it were the words: "Children are the new world. And all dreamers are children."

(During above, CUT TO: CLOSE-UP—The Statue of Liberty; then back to the ship's porthole. Visible in it is the excited face of Emma Goldman as a young woman. She turns into the cabin.)

EMMA: Helena! Helena! I can see it. Come quick!

(Helena comes up to the porthole. The two girls press their faces against it.)

EMMA: Dear sister. At last!

HELENA: Did you think it would be *green*?

EMMA: Oh yes—everything!

ABOUT THE AUTHOR

Martin Duberman is Distinguished Professor of History at Lehman College and the Graduate Center of The City University of New York. The author of thirteen books, he is the recipient of many prizes, including a special award from The National Academy of Arts and Letters for his "contributions to literature."

Duberman began his playwrighting career with *In White America*, which ran for a year and a half off Broadway, won the Vernon Rice/Drama Desk Award as the season's best play, had two national tours and also a variety of foreign productions. Among Duberman's subsequent plays are *Metaphors*, produced Off Broadway as part of *Collision Course*; *Dudes* at The New Dramatists and The Manhattan Theater Club; *The Memory Bank* at Tambellini's Gate; and *Visions of Kerouac*, commissioned by the Kennedy Center and produced at the Lion Theater Club in New York and the Odyssey Theater in Los Angeles. A volume of Duberman's plays have been collected in *Male Armor*.